Venetian Mirrors

Venetian Mirrors

JAKOB ZIGURAS
Foreword by David Bentley Hart

Angelico Press

First published in the USA
by Angelico Press 2024
Copyright © Angelico Press 2024

All rights reserved:
No part of this book may be reproduced or transmitted,
in any form or by any means, without permission

For information, address:
Angelico Press, Ltd.
169 Monitor St.
Brooklyn, NY 11222
www.angelicopress.com

ppr 978-1-62138-967-5
cloth 978-1-62138-968-2

Book and cover design
by Michael Schrauzer

History is a broken mirror, which reflects the image of God in man in a distorted and fragmented manner. The universal "apocatastasis" consists in restoring this integral image, in uniting its fragments for its definitive revelation beyond history.
— *Sergius Bulgakov*

Venice is first and foremost a literary and pictorial memory. The "vision" comes as a response to centuries of jottings and markings; what we see is the latest link in an endless chain of small equivalences, more or less compulsory thoughts, more or less exact translations.
— *Régis Debray*

I Mercury shine favourably on this above all other emporia.
— *Jacopo de' Barbari,* View of Venice

Contents

Foreword by David Bentley Hart   xv

1 Lazarus   2
2 The Drapery of Rain   4
3 Album Amicorum   6
4 Almost Venetian   8
5 The Drowned Moon   10
6 Lenten Dawn   12
7 The Vast Abandon   14
8 Icons   16
9 Beauty Without Debt   18
10 The Bees of Heaven   20
11 Wages of the Sea   22
12 I Gesuiti   24
13 The City Rising from the Sky   26
14 The Former Porousness   28
15 On Green Steps   30
16 A Profitable Franchise   32
17 A Piece of Lint   34
18 A Crumpled Handkerchief   36
19 A Shell Mosaic   38
20 The Threadbare Saraband   40
21 The Odour of Mythology   42
22 A Shade of Indecision   44
23 The Folk of Thresholds   46
24 Wunderkammer   48
25 A Bottomless Pastiche   50
26 Propitious Stars   52
27 Sere Corallum   54
28 A Minor Quay   56
29 The Fall of Dice   58
30 The Writhing Mesh   60

31 Her Limpid Privacy 62
32 An Upturned Helmet 64
33 The Lost Original 66
34 The Word Again 68
35 To Gnaw Upon Remains 70
36 The Lame Smith 72
37 A Waft of Ether 74
38 Santa Maria Nova 76
39 Patron of Corners 78
40 The Naked Masts 80
41 Between These Shores 82
42 Distinguished Graves 84
43 The Island of the Dead 86
44 A Taxonomy of Fates 88
45 The Mooring Lines 90
46 Sepia Pawnshop 92
47 A Faded Driftwood Chair 94
48 Pellestrina 96
49 Needle Lace 98
50 High Prattle 100
51 The Garish Show 104
52 The Ramifying Narrative 106
53 City of Misdirection 108
54 On the Margins 110
55 Other Portals Wait 112
56 Veritas 114
57 Games of Chance 116
58 The Veil Itself 118
59 The Poem Bleeds 120
60 Black Dog 122
61 The House of Craftsmanship 124
62 Spices from Acre 126
63 Mute Industry 128
64 The Palette of Diminished Greens 130
65 Foundation Mists 132
66 The Garbage Men 134

67	Discreet Amanuensis	136
68	A Bright Panache	138
69	The Masons of the Nameless Hand	140
70	A Nameless Epitaph	142
71	Written on a Tamarind	144
72	A Dive Bar Stage	146
73	The Ruin of Your Form	148
74	The Chained Blue Door	150
75	Sei Tornato	152
76	Flâneur	154
77	Atlantis Waiting	156
78	A Perfumery of Moods	158
79	Shallow Recollections	160
80	Without Face	162
81	Purgatorio	164
82	A Patient Breeze	166
83	A Winning Streak	168
84	An Open World	170
85	The Mall at Night	172
86	Discriminating Eyes	174
87	Elvis	176
88	Dottore, Dottore	178
89	Ospedale al Mare	180
90	Ghosts of Carnival	182
91	The Junk Armada	184
92	Weaving the Veils	186
93	The Smallest Crumb	188
94	Image Filter	190
95	Emerald Tablet	192
96	A Roaring Shell	194
97	Fabric Scraps	196
98	Narratives of Fate	198
99	Shuffling Masks	200
100	A Blink	202
101	Rooms of Mannequins	206
102	Convalescent Lovers	208

103 First View 210
104 Married to Water 212
105 Metropole 214
106 The Fledgling Dead 216
107 The Tryst 218
108 Dredgings 220
109 A Spotless Mirror 222
110 Ordinary Streets 224
111 A Shrine in Plastic 226
112 The Foundling Voices 228
113 Nono, Das atmende Klarsein 230
114 La Fabbrica Illuminata 232
115 The Shifting Context 234
116 The Hazy Light 236
117 A Great Star 238
118 A Double Feature 240
119 De Saliba, Annunciata 242
120 Drab Ecstasies 244
121 Giorgione, The Tempest 246
122 Veronese, The Feast in the House of Levi 248
123 Fecit, Fecit 250
124 Towards an Image 252
125 Brittle Larva 254
126 Pavilions 256
127 The Barnacled Colossus 258
128 The Crystal Trembles 260
129 An Endless Catalogue 262
130 The Surface 264
131 O Sulamita 266
132 A Lady's Fan 268
133 The Tranquil Basin 270
134 Dottor Serafico 272
135 Self-Portrait 274
136 The Voices of the Dead 276
137 The Street of Smoke 278
138 Unfocused Glance 280

139　The Sudden Absence　282
140　The Aldine Press　284
141　The Friday Book　286
142　A Gondellied　288
143　The Blush of Art　290
144　The Marble Body　292
145　Broken at the Feast　294
146　La Veneziana　296
147　A Dangerous Encounter　298
148　The Same Motif　300
149　The Jumble Sale　302
150　His Other Body　304
151　A Mountain Cure　306
152　Abandoned Wards　307
153　One More Round　308
154　The Perfect Work　309
155　A Festival of Failure　310
156　The Mushroom Pickers　311
157　The Cinema　312
158　Hans Castorp　313
159　Flakes of Skin　314
160　Disfigured Statues　315
161　It Drifts Away　316
162　Beyond All Storms　317
163　Notes　318
164　Acknowledgements　322

Foreword
BY DAVID BENTLEY HART

THE ONE GREAT DREAM THAT HAS PREOCCUPIED the mind of the West for going on two and a half millennia is Platonism. No other vision of reality, however powerful, has ever truly rivalled its claim upon the culture's spiritual imagination; and, no matter how often we imagine we have finally awakened from that dream, it is always still there waiting for us when we close our eyes and lay down our heads again. Sometimes it has been deep and replenishing, sometimes fitful and haunted by anxieties, but in its every form it has been marked simultaneously by both elation and melancholy. In its more sanguine, more orthodox expressions, it assures us of the reality of some other, better region "there above" where all the fleeting things we love "here below" have their eternal truth, untouched by the shadows of transience and death. In its more somber and heterodox expressions, it is pervaded by an Orphic or Gnostic pathos, a tragic sense of the terrible distance separating this world from that unimaginable realm of light. Sometimes it inspires us with an ecstatic longing for the vision of the eternal ideas in their original purity; sometimes it torments us with a sense of their unattainability. Sometimes it enchants us with the changeless beauty whose reflections fill this world; sometimes it oppresses us with a sense of how deeply disfigured that beauty has become in the dark mirror of matter and time.

I do not want, though, to give the impression that *Venetian Mirrors* is simply a book about Platonism. It is not simply *about* any one thing at all, as it is not a treatise, but rather a long and often haunting poetic sequence whose unifying logic is as much the consistency of its dreamlike flow as any conceptual "plot." Its constantly shifting images and interweaving themes advance no single discursive agenda, and whatever itinerary the book might follow is rather like the pattern of the city in which it is set, where one can quickly become lost in a labyrinth of sinuously winding streets and canals only to find oneself at some corner off its thoroughfares that seems still to be set in one or another earlier age. But, even so, there is a definite Platonic logic to all of the book's recurring motifs and conceits. (Or perhaps, for someone familiar with something of Ziguras's intellectual interests, one might call it a Sophiological logic, simply to take account of one of the styles of specifically Christian Platonism on which it draws.) And Venice, of course, is the perfect symbolic embodiment of the relation between an order of ideas "there above" and a disordered region of simulacra "here below," as well as of the *metaxy* where the two are indissolubly joined: a city, that is, in which a higher realm of radiant and stable forms is forever being at once captured and distorted in a formless and obscure lower realm of darkness and change. The device that gives the book its strange and entrancing effect, moreover, is its ingenious representation in the structure of the verse of Venice's play of reflections: on facing pages, each poem appears first in its "ideal" shape as a work of impeccably formal (and predictably beautiful) verse and then in its fluid, fragmented, mutable, and obscurely "distorted" reflection as a free, almost stream-of-consciousness rearrangement (without a single addition or subtraction) of the words and parts of words and even in some cases the letters from which the original verse was composed.

Ziguras has told me that he produced a good deal of this rearrangement by hand, even in many cases (in good William Burroughs fashion) cutting the original poems into pieces and then assembling them in new configurations on a table. His aim in doing so was to generate an effect analogous to Venice's reflected images of a solid world above in the constantly altering flow of the canals' waters below. It also at times produces a kind of delirious or dreamlike atmosphere, in which sense and nonsense intermingle, and each somehow constantly emerges from the other. So, too, the lucidity of true imagination and the disorientation of enchanting illusion continuously blend and separate and blend again. So, too, the historical and the fictional. Time's limits also occasionally melt away in such a way that the specular logic of the book is deepened by the mirroring of one of the city's epochs in another, as when Gaspara Stampa watches Rainer Maria Rilke across a canal, from the opposite end of one and the same bridge. In all the poems, moreover, in both their stable and their "deliquescent" forms, a variety of voices are audible, some dulcet and some jarring and many in between. These differences in tone become especially acute, perhaps, in the book's meditations upon the connections of the poetic imagination to that most Platonic of the soul's energies, eros, which the poems often explore in terms both exalted and deformed. There are visions of heavenly love in these pages, or at least its reflections, but also of that love's skulking incognito in the homelier and more ambiguous desires that wander through the city streets, which are occasionally reminiscent of a more Baudelairean urban landscape.

I should not go on, however. I do not believe in long introductions to good books, and I am especially hostile to the practice of joining long disquisitions in prose to books of poetry. Let me simply close, then, by noting something that does not need to be noted. Here, as in his previous original collections and translations, Ziguras distinguishes himself as a poet whose verse not only exhibits remarkable craftsmanship, but also shines with a very real and often mysterious beauty. As a single unified work, this book clearly far surpasses in technical and aesthetic ambitions anything he has previously produced; but it is no great surprise that it succeeds so singularly well and leaves behind so lingering an effect. This is the work of a fine artist at the height of his powers, and it is a genuine joy to be the one who gets to break a bottle of champagne on its prow, so to speak, as it is sent out upon the waters.

PART ONE

The Divine Sophia became also the creaturely Sophia.
God repeated Himself in creation, so to speak;
He reflected Himself in nonbeing.
— *Sergius Bulgakov*

But the souls of men see their images as if in the mirror
of Dionysus and come to be on that level with a leap
from above: but even these are not cut off from their
own principle and from Intellect.
— *Plotinus*

The world, like Dionysus, is torn to pieces by pure intellect,
but the Poet is Zeus; he has swallowed the heart of the world;
and he can reproduce it in a living body.
— *Owen Barfield*

1. Lazarus

I will not go to Venice, not this year—
no month in Venice, in this year of plague.
The beauty that would save remains a vague
appeal to Lazarus asleep; his bier

is borne on water—purified by lack
of tourists snapping at the corpse like crows—
on tears He also wept whose Spirit blows,
calls out *Come forth!* and calls the sleeper back.

As through that emptied city, my face masked
with grave-cloth to restrain the fetid breath
we share in every word—the prose of death—
I heed the Word for which the sisters asked.

For beauty waits, having once wiped His feet
with flowing hair, and grieving stands outside;
for beauty speaks the stench of him who died,
anointing with the fragrance of defeat.

Year to year, my tourist feet would go for a month: of Venice asleep in Venice, spirit emptied on water, beauty for beauty grieving. The city, masked by vague prose, also waits for His appeal; will, once purified through the fragrance that remains on this flowing cloth, share in the beauty that stands forth in Him who died to defeat death, asked breath to come and save the face of every word born of this snapping grave, restrain the not outside, which is as lack. He wept—anointing the corpse we the sleeper heed like crows aired stench of plague calls—The Word, whose back whip blows tear. No having sates. With rests With With and Is. Not I, His I speaks, calls Lazarus out of the fetid bier.

2. The Drapery of Rain

Pause by the bend of some canal, obscure
enough to part the drapery of rain,
watched by the plaster, placid Marian
shrines hung at corners, near a boarded door.

Across the tarry water, perched above
a garden wall, a glass-house balcony
observes the hours: faceless, solitary.
Someone before you dropped a crimson glove,

made of the cheapest lace, on mossy steps
right at the water where the slinky rats
hurry like waiters. Sometimes, weathered slats
on poster-plastered fences offer gaps

that give onto a lot, by rampant grass
and thistles overgrown, where one bent tree
begs for a few leaves like an amputee;
the ground: confetti, butts and broken glass.

Perched above the cheapest door overgrown by rampant drapery, a plaster amputee observes the garden, the crimson tree watched by a faceless pause. Someone, on a balcony, dropped glove, butts and confetti onto the broken steps. That lot of like-enough tropes corners and rats on you. Thistles, slats, fences, wall, obscure the solitary house bent before the glass at a bend of water, where placid mossy hours tarry, offer some weathered lace hung right near glass shrines to rain—where, sometimes, grass made of gaps begs the one ground given for the like part. Slinky leaves boarded at a canal marina, a few plastered waiters hurry by across the water.

3. Album Amicorum

Sober as Shakespeare writing down his will,
the sun forgets the bodies on the stage
and walks across the surface of the page.
While foreign men of substance stride and fill

an *album amicorum*, on the way,
with scraps of wisdom, noble signatures,
taxonomies recording what allures,
the floating costume's species of display.

Some pages are left blank, anticipate
the final costume, *bound in no bouquet*,
the shimmering of many in one sway
of cloth where constellations scintillate.

When will the portly merchant rest his feet—
his books complete, the influx free of duty—
be married indissolubly to beauty?
Not yet, not yet, the prostrate waves repeat.

Substances sway, yet rest. Shimmering signatures of wisdom. The floating constellations stride down, in noble costume and on foam feet. The ash merchant displays foreign species in his columbarium. The waves are left on the stage, when one forgets the final bodies portly men of the cloth will not anticipate: beauty's bouquet, the free influx of the city of surface where the yet-to-be scintillate. Many pages repeat the book. An admirer of His way walks across, while no *what* allures. The speaker, sober, duty-bound—with complete taxonomies, note-writing and recording of crap—will prostrate, as some blank page the sun fills.

4. Almost Venetian

Midnight in Venice (it's a wooden name,
you know, for this mingling with mist, reclined
on cafe cane-chairs, timelines intertwined).
All this is woven by that lowly Dame,

who drags Her robes of sea silk in the murk
of shallow puddles rising from the drains.
Antigone knelt down among remains;
the culmination of a finished work,

not saved in texture of a tapestry
but straining forward, silken veins of thought
that bind it to the burden strung out taut
towards the river's distant estuary —

like Volga boatmen, Repin's strokes release
to haul their golden barge in light *almost
Venetian*. Dawn lifts up its bloody host;
polluted waves pass on the sign of peace.

Peace, Who made It, for It knelt far out among waves, at the midnight that drains all signs of their light—His name woven in murk of river, mingling with the tapestry of timelines, to know cane-strokes, veins straining, strung up bloody from the finished work *Charis* lifts. Wooden remains, reclined down in the taut *not*, ripen to release the saved faces rising towards that distant culmination. On thought's lowly estuary: dawn drags her burden of golden robes; hosts of the sea pass in polluted shallow puddles; almost gone, boatmen on a barge rue a haul of mist. But, by this Word You bind it—vain gloat—in text intertwined like Venetian Venice, silken silk.

5. The Drowned Moon

The murky glass of the canal reflects
an ageing beauty, skin of curdled milk,
but draped with perfume and the evening's silk.
Her heavy tongue half-drunkenly inflects

the jealous waves that, for an age, have lapped
all Latin rigour from the floating streets.
Still dangerous, but tired of conceits,
of all her stratagems — a spider trapped

in her constructions, in her sticky webs —
she reads old letters: thinly veiled lust
of courtly suitors who have gone to dust.
A dark tide rises, while her body ebbs.

This is her death mask: pale and elegant;
the drowned moon bobs as plague-masked gondoliers,
wrapped in the night's *tabarro*, ferry fears.
The Carnevale always ends with Lent.

Veiled in an old silk, the elegant streets have gone to Carnevale—draped with death, wrapped with conceits and floating perfume. The curdled moon (all of her pale, jealous, but courtly suitors have lapped the milk waves of her body) reflects her tired age in lust for rigour, all Latin dust, an always still beauty, trapped in glass webs. A tongue of plague inflects as sticky stratagems. The canal ebbs from all her drowned gondoliers. She fears ageing, ends, reads the murky tide of letters that night's lent her: the half-dangerous constructions of a spider—who rises, dark and thinly masked. This evening's heavy tabarro is her skin, while the mask-ferry bobs, drunkenly.

6. Lenten Dawn

A smeared veneer of rain, a single star.
The polished street has pools of silverplate,
reflecting photographs of real estate.
Jazz slurs a solo at the locals bar.

The wind that drew the clouds no longer stirs
cold dregs of darkness in a coffee cup.
A tired waitress sweeps the glitter up.
An ancient huntress passes in her furs

perfumed with mothballs. The tableaux presents
a scene of *visionary dreariness*—
the neon viscera of Marsyas,
as pale Apollo cleans his instruments.

Tomorrow morning, monumental doors
thrown open by a brisk, indentured maid,
will let the light in, while the puddles fade
as Lenten dawn inclines to kiss the sores.

Rain, in a brisk jazz glitter, sweeps at puddles cold as morning, polished up by a visionary veneer of mists unrent, monumental clouds indentured to the pale estate of dawn. A silverplate tomorrow, a tableaux of smeared dregs, slurs the Real. An ancient huntress passes the neon pools, reflecting a waitress that cleans the bar, stirs coffee. The Star-Maid, thrown in darkness, inclines her cup. While Marsyas, perfumed with viscera, presents the will, the single dreariness of Apollo: his Lenten photographs a tired ash light drew, as a street scene. No wind. The balm of sloth. The locals in solo furs kiss, let the open doors of sores fade longer.

7. The Vast Abandon

At last a place with windows—three that gaze
upon their shared and inner blue abyss;
like fabric-roses in the corner, bliss
is but an image of their cloudless blaze.

Like wet sheets steaming in the midday sun
the things outside exhale their images;
inside is warm, secured from damages,
and the air-freshener is always on.

The carpet is a viscous olive green,
unmarked by wake of any slender boat.
The middling pastel paintings seem to float
like icons clicked and dragged across a screen.

At times you have to draw the paper shades
to veil the vast abandon of the sky,
in that memorial moment petrify
each unbegotten thing before it fades.

In middling pastel times that damages have secured,
You draw each thing's last cloudless image upon the
blue screen of the moment — a vast veil that fades.
Warm shades, their gaze dragged across paintings,
exhale at midday, steaming before icons: windows
to the blaze of the begotten Sun, inviolate atoner.
Float on the abyss of the inner sky, by slender
green boat. Inside, like outside, images their bliss —
the Three, always awake in their shared abandon.
Unmarked paper is a memorial from the place
unlike anything. The corner roses seem wet and
viscous, freshen air and petrify, to carpet fabric
with sheets. But it clicked: Is Is like Is and...

8. Icons

Like gymnasts' ribbons, each a signature
cursive through time, the body's silken sash...
A hot wind blows these trembling gods, like trash,
towards the tip where everything impure,

lit by its image, burns up from within:
resplendent in abjection, saved by fire—
desire turned to ash by pure desire—
Gehenna lit up, incandescent skin.

Dry breath of summer. Brittle hearts and dry
kindling of kinship, gathered on the plane
of immanence, find they cannot contain
the blaze of life that burns in drawing nigh

and all the city's windows sets aflame
with gold like icons of another world,
into whose furnace everything is hurled—
representation beyond any frame.

She cannot find whose twisty desire hurled everything resplendent into the hot, dry ash-tip of Gehenna, to kill it. The abjection of representation. Breath, pure beyond brittle worlds, trembling within a silken furnace of desire — everything turned by icons, hearts' incandescent windows, aflame in and saved through that Body's immanence. Dry wind blows; by its cursive ribbon the image is gathered: gods drawing in ash, skin, each signature, another gold city, towards a kindling blaze of kinship. The trash-fire time lit — impure summer, where like burns up like, nigh on the plane these forms frame, contain — by life burns up. The mystes sang of any and all.

9. Beauty Without Debt

This fish-bowl palace, with its shallow moat,
will fall at last before the wordless roar,
as beards of salt and foam reclaim the shore.
On other waters will that city float,

which bodies forth the sky without a tain—
serene as only beauty without debt
when all mere mirrors, unregenerate,
dissolve and only images remain.

All furled desire rendered explicate
and endlessly unfolding, without thorn
to mar the stem from which the rose is born;
and all the letters of the alphabet

repeat one Word, but differently each time—
like margins in a hymnal that reclaim
at last with leaf the ruins of a name—
all in agreement, as in perfect rhyme.

Without bodies, all remain shallow in the wordless roar of perfect agreement, furled as one. Each, when with and without time born in the Word, leafs at last with letters of its regenerate name, repeats the fall differently. Serene fish, on the shore of the sky. Before all mirrors and endlessly unfolding water, without which all this which floats is only tainmare, images-in-debt rhyme at the thorn margin. Unlike the city desire foams to reclaim rendered forth as salt, but as a hymnal alphabet beauty rose from a palace ruin. Only dissolve, Bard, that last atom, stem that other will, and a mere bowl will explicate and reclaim the All.

10. The Bees of Heaven

The lanterns are barbaric samovars,
suspended from the domes on chains of thorns.
The Pantocrator rules beyond the stars.
Too real, the pixelated gold adorns

the cupolas besmirched by clouds of myrrh
and frankincense. A church of smoky wax.
You can't help trembling and the photos blur.
A splendid doorway guards the golden pyx:

in front the saints, with wings of peeling leaf,
conceal the jewel-encrusted opulence
behind the pallid frescos of belief,
beyond the smutty majesty of sense.

Below the prophets on the altar dome,
the bees of heaven buzz, as one, the Name,
imprisoned in their priceless honeycomb,
or harvest swaying fields of candle flame.

Bees buzz, as prophets of the honeycomb; wings blur and harvest the beyond. Pallid guards, by the doorway of belief, with a candle help the besmirched senses. The stars are lanterns, suspended on the dome of the pyx, of the golden heaven. The church and the cupolas too, a majesty of myrrh, can't conceal You, the one priceless jewel beyond opulence, Name behind smoky clouds from the altar. Below, barbaric samovars, on the fields of the front. Imprisoned in splendid frescoes or the frank incense of swaying pixelated domes, smutty wax encrusted photos — saints; chains of flame adorn their gold leaf peeling. The Pantocrator rules, trembling in real thorns.

11. Wages of the Sea

Their influence is Macedonian:
the hidden frescoes in the baptistery
discovered first in 1963,
after *the end of the "Chatterley" ban*...

Which was eight centuries too late for me,
one angel thinks, his body a grey blur.
Although they lift their hems, the saints incur
the impure, lacy wages of the sea.

Beneath their marble blankets having lain
(which proved too short to shield their naked feet),
they woke like lovers, netted in a sheet,
embarrassed by the very patent stain.

Thus, accidentally, are all things restored;
revealed while working on another task.
The unknown God removes His tragic mask,
reveals the pallid handmaid of the Lord.

Thus, the unknown Handmaid, working for centuries on the naked marble beneath which the first lovers are hidden, removes one pallid mask after another, lifts the ban, reveals the wages of ire they accidentally incur. Although they discovered the I—woke late, by a sea netted, their Lord-like task a blur—the grey alley-chatter, very patent, was too short to influence the Macedonian. While the angel—in sheet, shield, lacy hem—thinks their feet impure, God, 1 in 3, His bare pity revealed is all embarrassed things (the 99, me too), having restored His body of saints, proved the end of the tragic stain, which blankets their frescoes in night.

12. I Gesuiti

The church, near a blind doorway's abstract plaque—
Ruskin consigned it among those whose ilk
delight in marble made to look like silk—
drapes toppled stone in table-cloth Baroque.

This is where Ignatius Loyola
and friends, when ordained to the priestly task,
knelt to attention. The inlaid damask
hangs like wallpaper plastered with a roller.

Far-off, the Solomonic columns swirl
like stone tornadoes, with a graphite sheen;
up close they scintillate in blue and green.
Above, the lesser-known Selaphiel

dispels the incensed words round those who pray,
that they might only frost the stone-cold air—
suspend a light-refracting chandelier,
beneath a gilded shell by Fabergé.

Refracting in the frost chandelier, they knelt like a toppled column, to pray to the far blue, to beg fear; they, laid in piles among cold shells, swirl like silk tornadoes, whose cloth drapes that abstract stone doorway with a gilded marble plaque. Where the *Da* is mask-off, the close air incensed to dispel it, might heal those consigned scintillae. Those moon coils roll round, suspend this graph paper and stone wall, when in a barque-like green church, with only a stone table, Ruskin, Loyola—sheen-plastered, blind—look up to the priestly task. The I, Who hangs near us—above and beneath the made, known by attention like light—delights in lesser, iterating words, ordained as friends.

13. The City Rising from the Sky

A mausoleum for the hallowed dead—
their meat kept fresh inside this marble fridge.
The festival involved a pontoon-bridge,
till industry put childish fun to bed.

It's like a bad tooth, when the gum recedes.
The joints, between the letters of the vow,
filled up with earth-like sediment that now
began to sprout forth in abundant weeds.

The statue on the summit of the dome,
Christ the Redeemer (made of puppet wood,
recycled mannequins), restored for good,
stands on this sea-shell that had humbled foam

(though at some cost, since Titian had to die),
with sheets of lead nailed to His wooden form,
pointing the way with His replacement arm
towards the city rising from the sky.

Though childish, marble mannequins foam of their replacement, pointing at the restored mausoleum dome, way on the summit of noon, like a tooth—with some lead statue hallowed, with the abundant festival of recycled meat, the industry involved to arm the dead, that began to shell the city. Since the cost of joint fun had between the sheets, atop this wood bed, recedes, die with the bad puppet; that fort-like mug, rising toward the Good had inside the filled Now, puts on Christ, when His form—humbled, nailed to the wooden letters (sea, earth, sky) I taint for a fridge, stands up from this sediment. The Redeemer sprouts fresh in weeds, to bridge till his vow, made, is kept.

14. The Former Porousness

A pallid rose, she is indeed *formosa*
this morning: steeple like a plaster cast,
the dustmen, with their burden, pushing past.
Fresh produce, fondled by a fat greengrocer,

remains untouched in patient ripening
in its own garden, behind every wall.
Come straight from hunting-lodge to market stall,
the changeling heads still glitter as they swing.

Diminished, yes; the former porousness —
when, soft as honeycomb, each silent cell
recited psalms of sunlit dust, a bell,
the heart would call the scattered mind to Mass —

has, like a shark's egg, withered into this
papier-mâché of presence, chalked with salt
left on the tongue's coast like an ancient fault.
Thought must free-dive to pry the pearls of bliss.

The former garden, in deed past; the ancient morning ripening like a rose, untouched by fault, scattered like remains. Diminished dustmen, pushing plaster produce, each in their own cell, with heads chalked, recited withered pearls of thought. Ache is the massy wall of mind fondled, as psalms stall on this paper coast — fat sharks of the free market hunting. She still calls, as pallid sunlit honeycomb. I salt an egg, cast a glitter, dive into a changeling porousness, every straight steeple a yes to this dust left behind. When the cog would err (it has to) pray with them to swing bell-like, heart, lodge in silent bliss the tongue's green burden — so, from patient presence a soft fresh form must come.

15. On Green Steps

A church of terracotta—marked with chalk,
and with severest cypress tree gravure—
beside a schoolyard where the children roar
like crayon daisies, too replete to talk.

Sunlight bisects the court; the rusted hoop,
hung at one end—a broken fishing net—
is pencilled on the asphalt. You forget
where you were bound. Reclining on a stoop,

one of the homeless leant against a vast
library door, to hear the whispering
of books like courtiers before a king.
The last shall be the first, and the first last.

Early this morning, on the Piazzetta,
you sat on green steps—where the vessels clink
against their images—and wrote, *I think*...
pilfering bandwidth to compose a letter.

Broken vessels — before, children of the morning court, green images — hear the whispering asp, pilfering, stoop too early, forget the replete Ur-I, beside and one with the One, first and last, bound to the books you wrote, hung on the tree, reclining on the vast grave their halt, homeless step compose (the clink, where the marked on the tiers, the yard, talk, pencil *to be*, chalk I-asides, leant against a rusted church door; where sects think to hoop you with crayon, first letter of a library, net you, King Fish attracting roe) — led at last where severest sunlight shall bisect and end the school of like against like.

16. A Profitable Franchise

Charon has many ferries in this town:
a profitable franchise (plutocrats
prefer their motor-launches). Water rats
paddle through the mirror, upside down.

The dead, like cattle, jostle at the docks.
Some, laid already in the lacquered shells
of open mussels (oozing carnal smells),
ignore the booming of the polished clocks —

the tall, mechanic patriarchs of time.
The surface closes where the prows have passed:
the silvery reverse of now, the past
where presence gathers — ornamental rime.

They trail their fingers in mortality
and barely note the showmanship of mist,
as silent as a skilled illusionist
erasing the facades of memory.

Note the facades that jostle like cattle, and the silvery patriarchs erasing mortality. Ignore their booming presence, where the past closes this profitable mirror. Charon has silent fingers, and the barely-open carnal mussels — in lacquered prows of the dead — paddle in the docks of memory. Tall plutocrats prefer the smells and surface of now. Time launches a polished franchise in this town (many mechanic rats already at the reverse of showmanship). Some illusionist gathers clocks oozing mist, as skilled ferries motor through the upside-down water, the ornamental trail of rime laid where their shells have passed.

17. A Piece of Lint

The shadows wane, as did the Doge's own;
enter a Logue-like epic, turn the page —
eclipsed in signs APOLLO, come in rage,
turns all the pages after white as bone.

Bridges of sense span broken hemispheres;
like truffle — plush, metallic on the tongue —
you taste bells by no living ringer rung,
you hear the flaking eczema as the years

flake off a wall: a quote, the poet's dates
are all that mark his former residence.
In empty barracks foreign soldiers fence.
Or are they waiters, with the empty plates

on which our bright utensils clink and glint?
Settle the bill, put on your coat, then stand
and touch the clouds of heaven, with numb hand,
inside your pocket like a piece of lint.

Are you His, like the hermit, or your own, like the dud, empty, foreign you (your ringer) put by, inside the plush clink, which turns from the lit wall flaking like eczema. As rage wanes, spheres turn and ruffle. Broken, metallic soldiers settle in shadow barracks. The poets in residence are of a piece. Apollo's waiters enter on cue, with plate and bill, then pocket a quote they fence after. Log off, on Dogen's page; span the All on tensile glint-bridges no dates mark. Signs stand on the years' rungs, touch the bright white clouds. Come, taste — with a tongue numb and empty as bone — heaven in that flake of living pages: the epic of sense eclipsed, as all at the hour hear the bells.

18. A Crumpled Handkerchief

A folding picture post-card, self-contained,
replete with pleats like a Miyake dress,
the old accordion of endlessness
time plays to keep the pilgrims entertained—

the city swells with tides as it inhales,
holding the past up to a trembling nose:
a crumpled handkerchief that saves a rose
ever unfolding into fragrant veils.

Where two streets intersect, you think you see
the one you chose, but did not choose again:
the first mirage to haunt the desert plain
of unrepeatable identity.

The flow is constant; new crusaders wait
to sail for Elsewhere—the impregnable
iconoclastic city with its wall
through which all enter by the same blank gate.

O impregnable Rose in a desert of trembling endlessness — the same replete One, folding as unrepeatable, new but alike, pleats. Time did not see the first picture crumpled. To enter the fragrant handkerchief, choose a blank constant mirage, entertained by the iconoclastic wall that plays dress up with veils; a/the post-city pilgrims ever again think, inhales a past city which haunts it. You intersect with the plain old flow, sail the tides of elsewhere. Card-holding crusaders swell through two streets, to the gate — you its key. You chose accord, to wait with the self-contained saves — where the aim for all *noes* is to keep unfolding into identity.

19. A Shell Mosaic

The sea of molten glass descends to form:
a gaudy, crystal trinket in the hand.
The foam of Venus now pollutes the strand;
used condoms ooze like slugs after a storm.

This wrack, whose chains lie rusting on a beach—
a shell mosaic or a cento made
of saturated phrases that will fade
the moment they are lifted into speech—

is what is salvaged from the muddy flow
of images: mere drafts of afterwords
(each grey conspectus, cobbled afterwards)
to the *annotated archipelago*.

These narrow channels, dammed and drained, reveal
the merchant captain's thousand wooden legs—
he drank the turbid port down to the dregs—
to dredge what pearls there may be left to steal.

Thousands storm the beach, to reveal — in a gaudy, saturated moment a slug caps — the form salvaged from the flow, afterwards annotated. They drank the turbid glass of Venus and fade, drained to mere images, to wrack on a strand of the grey sea, whose chains lie rusting, after the dregs (cobbled wooden legs or hands) ooze port. He will dredge this muddy speech; descends after these pearls — used words, drafts of the made — to steal what is left down there, that each arcane shell, like crystal concepts the tain's epoch pollutes, may be lifted out of the mood-foam (merchant phrases, narrow channels dammed, a trinket-cento) into the molten mosaic of what is now a Grail.

20. The Threadbare Saraband

The leaf of discourse climbs the villa wall;
its febrile tendrils feed on speechless air.
Dead flowers flourish in an atmosphere
as choked with waiting as an interval.

The peacock pâté served, the worthies dine:
impotent dandies, syphilitic dames,
stiletto-tongues with claims and counter-claims,
which the denouement renders anodyne.

They plant their stakes within a boggy strand,
admire themselves in mirrors' shallow streams,
apply their costly unguents and creams
and dance upon the threadbare Saraband.

Blood streaks the marvel of the marble floor,
inside the future's empty embassies.
Desires are already memories.
The old men vaunt under Medusa's stare.

In the embassies, as they feed the peacock, which renders villa air costly with its flourish, memory is choked with the pith of Sicily. Medusa's febrile dames, their tendrils, speechless tongues, dance an impotent stiletto saraband upon the mirror's shallow dead. Desire already streaks the marble floor, inside the future's empty pate. An atmosphere of threadbare denouement, as worthies admire the dandies on stakes, stare and apply creams, vaunt their old boggy claims, in a sung-tune marvel. The discourse served under counter-claims; the blood streams and climbs within plant, leaf, flowers, and men themselves, waiting, stranded in the anodyne interval.

21. The Odour of Mythology

A smoking man attempts to brush the ash
that falls upon his freshly dry-cleaned suit;
thus life burns down, deposits flakes of guilt
and stains the fingers. Fire first, then trash.

A *pescaria* worker shovels ice;
the smell is pungent, catches like a hook—
your nostril forcing you, despite the snook,
to trace the briny contours of a place

where blood glints on the mail of infantry
Poseidon raised against invading fleets,
still vowing to repay his past defeats—
the iron odour of mythology

kept fresh by crystals, which the winter frost
prevents from melting. The enamel eyes
of fish enclose marine hostilities;
the war continues, though the battle's lost.

Despite battle's oak, shovels forcing down the guilt, Your fresh blood, like Isaac's, stains the fall's lost mythology. War catches hook-fingers on the fish mail (glint of the first winter, frost's crystal trace) invading a place of ash and trash, contours that burn from the eyes of the smoking iron-man, raised to continue hostilities against flakes freshly melting. Ice deposits, attempts to enclose fleet life; whereupon, His brush—though still—as fire defeats briny infantry. Poseidon is cleaned of the past marine enamel, by prior dry Lents, which repay the kept odour, the pungent smell of it, the worker as His; thus vowing, then, the Son presents us to You.

22. A Shade of Indecision

You never know which narrow wound's a path
into an empty courtyard, where a bird
repeats the same melodious foreign word,
in a cage covered by a sun-bleached cloth,

and which to a familiar cul-de-sac
stinking of urine, with a post-box full
of unread letters and promotional
leaflets and catalogues. While, turning back

to see if your soul follows close behind,
will only cause it to withdraw, a shade
of indecision. In this pasquinade,
your hunchbacked shadow mocks the regal mind.

Best lose your way completely, till of grief
not even the most muffled footstep falls,
as speechless night paces her marble halls,
black-lace *moretta* clenched in pearl-white teeth.

Mind, clothed in mock-decision, hunched in a stinking cage, with a foot taps at letters (and a box of sun-bleached, post-Aquinas leaflets, unread), paces urine-covered catalogues, full of familiar promotional teeth. Withdraw your wound's foreign grief, clenched soul, which follows a speechless path; till, completely empty of cause — and behind your will to know — you see the same, if most regal, Pearl, close in this best black night, and Her melodious marble hall, where a white bird repeats a lace-muffled word, by a courtyard into which the shadow never falls. While turning back to the shade, lose not only footsteps in a narrow cul-de-sac, even more — your way back in.

23. The Folk of Thresholds

On flotsam stilts, in white, Felliniesque,
posing beside a doorway, finely draped,
beside two children who have just escaped
out from the foldings of their lustrous damask —

the folk of thresholds wave across the dim,
duskened canal, as a magnesium flash
freezes the shuffling celluloid of flesh.
Only the long craft, everlasting, skim;

only the sea receives what they inscribe.
Only they move; all else: a grey relief,
Christ crucified, and the repentant thief.
And, in a puff of fog, that ruddy tribe

are gone, as candles sputter, but persist,
in minor shrines. The weathered candy-canes
map each ancestral channel that remains,
leaning askew against the coming mist.

But the two, only as children, posing askew in and out of the ancestral doorway, they have duskened the lustrous everlasting flesh—Christ. What else remains of their flotsam? Weathered damask shrines, minor thresholds. On stilts, the long-folk puff the grey fog, sputter, are gone. In the dim relief beside the Crucified, repentant candles, leaning, flash against foldings of shuffling mist. A magnesium-draped thief, who only just escaped from the map, freezes beside a celluloid canal that receives only the white skim of a sea. The coming tribe, ruddy as candy, move Felliniesque across a wave; they persist, channel the craft, inscribe finely in each and all.

24. Wunderkammer

In the complete collection, silver pins
arrest the iridescent carapace
of seconds feeding on the corpse of space—
an ark of single, barren specimens

afloat on formalin. The incomplete
collection stumbles, like an eager child,
towards its mother to be reconciled—
a graceful marionette on tender feet;

and each addition is repeatedly
inducted in a rite of solemn joy,
invested with the lofty rank of *toy*,
before a new election sets it free...

The total archive is the empty page
scarred by the scraping of a bone-dry pen,
unable to describe the madeleine
whose second taste confirms the golden age.

A scarred marionette, in the silver age, whose barren taste elides the Amen—invested in a collection of the collection of crap, unable to be, like the golden Child, second by no addition, to see graceful joy confirms the tender corpse, formal bones of lofty feet vain seconds arrest with pins—the single iridescent specimen stumbles, repeatedly, before the solemn rite is complete. Afloat in the mother, feeding on reconciled space, on the free and new. Inducted, empty of rank, each pen eager to sing of it, describe. A dry page is an incomplete lection towards the *Archē,* a carapace of stark totality.

25. A Bottomless Pastiche

It has been sinking since before before:
a stranded Argo—slowly ossified
in aeons past, when all the heroes died,
never regaining their paternal shore—

become a reef held hostage by the swish,
the lace ennui of sentimental tides,
beneath whose babble ghostly Byron rides
through congregations of myopic fish.

In sun-bleached cells, in every coral niche,
eroded saints, whom floating gulls attend,
sink down into reflections without end,
blending into a bottomless pastiche.

Flapping in flocks and bright as tropic birds,
street-sellers hope to satisfy the Fates.
In pregnant puddles semblance propagates,
and hands wear down the currency of words.

Eroded Argo, hostage in a reef of babble, without sentimental fates — sink through the street, beneath paternal words, never regaining hope whose bright cells held all stranded heroes. When the has-been Byron rides a sun sinking slowly down into bottomless puddles, attend: down in ghostly congregations of ennui, the swish lace-sellers — to whom, since it died, the End hands tropic semblance and propagates, as before, in myopic tides — before blending into their coral niche, become the saints of pastiche and wear down every ossified past and bleached currency. Birds in reflections and floating fish satisfy the flocks of pregnant aeons flapping down.

26. Propitious Stars

Crouched in the marshes, snaring water-birds.
The squelch of footsteps that at once recede.
The ever-shifting hunting grounds of need,
both tide and fog erasing tracks and words.

Knee-deep in mud, among the bamboo spears
mud-people wielded against Lombard hosts,
salt farmers gathering the yield of coasts,
with which to savour and preserve lean years.

The exarch exodus, on sandy bars—
a crippled people hobble past on stilts,
across a turbid battleground of silts,
trailing their nets to catch propitious stars—

into a mirror barnacles encrust.
You drown there too, hung in some shadowed hall,
or in the window of a shopping mall—
your flesh is but the glass, which holds the dust.

Mud-encrusted, you crouched and crippled flesh that holds spears against the dust-shadowed words of gathering, on grounds which yield to the hosts of the shifting deep. Some bamboo birds, in exodus across the glass battleground—years hobble their stilts. With the fog farmers, I wield trailing nets in turbid marshes; but, the too-lean stars recede. People hunting people in bars, drown, window shopping a mall mirror. On your knees, in the barnacle hall, erasing snaring mud of a past tide, preserve, Bard, the savour of salt and tracks of need among sandy coasts, or footsteps which squelch into propitious silts to catch the Everwater—hung there as X, both *Archē* and loam at once.

27. Sere Corallum

A slighted eunuch venomously smiles:
on stalls of glistening Adriatic wares,
upon the wave-gnawed alphabet of piles,
the brackish maze of muddy thoroughfares;

the windblown follies, lace of tidal froth
laid for a feast of histrionic glass,
riding the swell of Hun and Ostrogoth;
her sere corallum and the overpass

that drips clean blood into a withered vein
as Venice, nodding on her life support,
pays tribute to her grizzled suzerain,
with perfumed envoys from her squalid port.

He sees the fleet of dusk, the strongest locks
undone by rusty keys, the endless slump
of molten time—beneath a winking lamp,
Titian succumbing slowly to the pox.

O, Her endless, molten, perfumed alphabet, by a slump undone. And the support of brackish glass stalls Her sere Adriatic fleet. The strongest envoys to that Venice maze, go from port, succumb to wind-blown thoroughfares. Cue the grizzled Hun: hunting, riding upon the swell of froth, wave of follies, winking wares. A pile of pox, a withered feast, venomously glistening, slowly gnawed as he — slighted, histrionic Titan, thief of the nodding lamp — sees the lace corallum pass, over the tidal time of her life laid beneath. Dusk roosts with rusty keys, pays her blood tribute, for the suzerain's lean smile drips on and on into a squalid muddy vein of schlock.

28. A Minor Quay

Like glossy fish with bright, mosaic scales
that lie, eyes glazed, upon a slippery dock,
by rigging ticking like an antique clock —
the city rots beneath the swaying sails.

The light long gnawed this ornamental bone,
and now *stands famished among all his pasts.*
The wind plays flags between the clustered masts,
in variations on a monotone.

Slow the boats undulate: their lazy staves
rise and fall, tied up beside a minor quay;
transcribe the dark legato of the waves,
the sad decay of virtuosity

that builds — above the shallow, swampy drone —
a crumbling edifice of counterpoint.
The sun spills chrism, stooping to anoint
the moist brow of a Doge who dies alone.

Crumbling light stands stooping beneath mosaic eyes of glossy virtuosity. A sad wind plays among clustered bone. Alone, the Doge scales the swaying, slippery rigging of a lie, above lazy sails, a quay and long dock gnawed by the slow, shallow, famished waves. A sun, like a glazed and monotone clock that rots, spills upon the swampy city a dark, ornamental decay. All pasts undulate in minor variations. The bright Fish dies, tied up between the masts, beside the boats that anoint the glazed brow. Who builds, on the drone of the dark, with his chrism counterpoint, the now legato fall of this ticking edifice, to transcribe the rise of their flags' moist staves?

29. The Fall of Dice

The gambler on the threshold, mask in hand,
not yet committed to the fall of dice,
observes the silent pageantry of vice,
the mustered peacocks brandishing their fanned

facades of hazard—partial panoply,
apparel of apparent personhood,
action suspended in subjunctive mood
saving appearance of equality—

and tumbles into freedom with his pack
of tampered cards, buffoonery of wit.
Subversive revels void the State of shit.
His noble toga endless shades of black,

Gerachi kneels in sewage. Blindness stinks
of black; his honest essence is on view.
Only reflection cocks his name askew.
A mob guffaws at dwarves and mountebanks.

Essence tumbles into sewage—a mob of peacocks at the endless threshold of appearance. Freedom, the silent not-yet of subjunctive dice, saving the mood of equality. Action is partial blindness. The noble gambler—committed to his fall—stinks of personhood, his mask askew and name at hazard, facades in hand, panoply of fanned cards in view of the mustered shades, the honest mountebanks, guffaws of dwarves brandishing their cocks—apparent revels in the vice of the State. The wit Gerachi—buffoonery suspended on the void, subversive only in reflection—kneels in shit, wearing his black toga, observes the black pageantry of tampered apparel.

30. The Writhing Mesh

Marine contingencies enact a chance
of sinking into silence without trace:
the vast armada of the commonplace,
rare objects blown to please the king of France.

The turbid keratin of sunlit sails
resembles, as they rise and fall and sway
(the petals of the rose are peeled away),
an onion's pale, lachrymatory veils.

Each year the sea receives a fleet of naves.
The Pope removes his ring. The writhing mesh
of water and the Doge become one flesh.
He walks and calms the serpent of the waves.

The fibrous gore of victory could caulk
a while the gaps through which the people bled
to undermine the floating figurehead.
The last one ended as a prison hulk.

The commonplace hulk of the Fall sails the writhing petals of silence, the turbid sway of flesh, of water. The blown naves ring out with chance, while fibrous contingencies' fleet figurehead walks the keratin mesh of the waves, which could undermine the caulk of the gaps. The people, sinking, blend, become the pale objects they enact: an armada of veils, farce and gore. The marine pope calms the sea doge as he removes his lachrymatory tattoo. Each, in a floating prison, resembles a king, receives the one rare, sunlit year of the last victory. As the vast trace of a serpent, ended, the peeled onion's a rose. Away and through are one. Please nod and rise.

31. Her Limpid Privacy

Let her undress before the elders, stand
reflected in her limpid privacy,
dressed in the spoils of their piracy—
the human contours of a naked land.

Cartographers of custom would impose
their warp and weft on silk, wielding lorgnettes,
to demarcate the world in silhouettes,
raise walls against a rolling tide of clothes.

Ideas make their summer promenade,
under bright parasols of images;
high on their stilts, no water damages
their elderflower hems—so slow to fade—

whose latticed shadows have the musty smell
of lingerie the body has betrayed,
and only moths stroke. Precious words are weighed,
and every essence has a slave to sell.

So then, essence on stilts has reflected in a naked tide, rolling in to undress walls a lingerie of privacy has latticed. World, wielding Her bright contours of silk and custom, dressed in summer silhouettes — Her high hems stroke the water. Let the warp-cartographers stand against the musty fadeland piracy spoils, smell the weft of elder flowers before their clothes are on, and raise their weighed words — their every letter and song — to demarcate a promenade of precious damages, whose under-shadows would have only parasols to sell, their human body betrayed (slave of the elder moths). Slow images of ideas on the make impose their limp id.

32. An Upturned Helmet

An upturned helmet swallows wedding bands.
Ashes are not yet panned for golden teeth.
A mother, yoked beneath a soldier's wreath,
rebinds with rings of steel her sisters' hands.

The soil is washed by blood, the hands by toil
and soap that's free from all impurities:
palm oil from the English colonies
replaced by laurel or by olive oil.

Instead of sweets, boys fill their little sacks
with metal scrap that feeds the war machine.
Cribs take the place of bristly Nordic green.
All foreign furs are stripped from clothing racks.

But Mars is not without a sense of style;
Graces he favours have a lot to gain.
As Damerini said, *The war in Spain
brought us the charm of the Bolero.* Smile!

Her dais and clothing are golden, the smile is all teeth, the metal hands have rings; a bristly wreath of scrap graces Dame Style in Nordic furs. Yoked by her charm, Mars feeds the little swallows meat from a palm, instead of soap, oils the racks as sweet boys without hands gain the steel sisters' favours, toil a lot to fill sacks of ashes, are stripped, washed by foreign blood that rebinds all soldiers with their mother—that the wedding take place beneath a helmet of laurel. Cribs of sense and impurities oil the English machine.War.ini is not yet upturned by bands from pain's free colonies or replaced, by us, with an olive pen for all, green but brought from no soil. The bole rots.

33. The Lost Original

The Campanile casts a shadow—falls
across the square where imitation rules
the synchronised chorography of fishy schools,
divided by transparent intervals—

itself is shadowed by what it repeats:
the lost original no plans retain,
which only stands in being built again,
the always broken promise that the streets

might like a tangled fishing-net be laid
before the gaze with all their writhing haul.
Each moment, born inside a filmy caul,
delivered to the future, is remade

in its own image. The caretaker's cat
the only victim of the fall the law
com'era e dov'era would restore—
the endless ruin of the predicate.

Being, in the transparent original image, repeats itself, that endless predicate which the future always remade. The/a square stands divided. The law a ruin by a Nile camp. The filmy gaze, born inside each writhing moment, victim of no before, synchronised with its rathe fall — a cat lost in fishy streets. Only the Caretaker's own might, laid across the Fall's tangled shadow would, by fishing, cast to retain the net haul. Only what is built again rules all delivered, shadowed schools, where their imitation of the promise restores the caul, the broken interval's chorography. Come era of the Dove! The plan, be like it is!

34. The Word Again

You pass: a neon sign beneath an arch,
the Quadri (full of sullen Austrians)
and the Piazza where the cafe bands
play one unending military march;

the columns with their cobbled refugees
from Africa; the svelte and snowy craft
like Borzoi kennelled; a light pencil draft —
San Giorgio Maggiore; pleasantries

with Frau von Wallenberg, polite retreats
from long white gloves as sinuous as swans,
from waiters dancing like automatons.
Like cats in search of sunlit garden seats,

stray threads of jasmine vanish in the weft —
the death of flowers giving birth to lace —
as night picks up the chalk of Arthur Stace
and writes the word again, from right to left.

Borzoi, in the night garden full of stray jasmine; the sinuous cats vanish. On a sunlit Piazza—as polite military bands search and sign with chalk the van-kennelled refugees in unending march from death—svelte Giorgio writes columns again, and the Arch-Automatons pencil draft pleasantries beneath the flowers of neon one picks. From a long awful gun barrel, giving birth to Africa: white gloves, left with right dancing; the cafe Argo, where sullen Austrians play to rid the *as qua as* of enigmas— their waiters of cobbled caste. Arthur swans, sates, retreats from word-craft, from the light, lace weft of like, like, like . . . You—threads up the snowy pass . . .

35. To Gnaw Upon Remains

The *carovane* slide along their rails,
from theme-park ticket booth to ticket booth;
our feelers moist, we leave behind a sleuth
of moonlit slime like plump and homeless snails.

The peristalsis that processes taste:
along the glittering conveyor belt,
our casings stuffed with all we've seen and felt,
we shamble through time's shambles, with distaste

for all the other zombies being led
by dreamy hungers, and in want of brains,
who only kneel to gnaw upon remains
and act the part among the living dead

like method actors who, with growing dread,
hope they're the heroes of this genre piece.
And then, after self-consciousness — release.
St Mark's is like a shotgun to the head.

Our homeless hungers, they are like genre zombies this arcane sleuth marks with distaste and with shotgun casings. We leave dreamy slime — the method dread's belt, plump moonlit brain the ticket — living processes growing feelers felt slide from heroes to actors. The dead gnaw their moist piece of the Other, stuffed with want, and then shamble booth to glittering booth for a ticket behind the seen-weave. Only after, time nails upon being the fond hope or vow, Who among our like is and all along remains the lead theme, Who in and through parts (spirit lees) conveys release to St Act of Consciousness. By Thee, head Self, all kneel along like rails, taste that park's shambles.

36. The Lame Smith

The gate is guarded like Grecian villa
out in the suburbs. With his stone ears pinned,
one sheepish lion's being disciplined.
The pantheon could use some putty-filler

(their temenos fenced in with lozenge spears):
Athena leans beneath the Dante quote;
Apollo cocks his hip, his gaze remote;
while tinnitus roars in Poseidon's ears.

The lame smith? Missing, very likely drunk;
he hasn't worked for many centuries.
The bellows of the past now merely wheeze,
fanning the furnace that for ages stank

of boiling pitch and resin; now the breeze
wafts fruity arabesques of vaping-pens,
as youths in speed-boats sputtering like Stens
assert their own dominion of the seas.

Athena, vamping the centuries, very likely hasn't worked out. Some, drunk with the past, boast, sputtering like teens, assert dominion of the suburbs; lame pens merely quote fruity disciplined stone of the missing Grecian pantheon. The One now roars like lions for the tin ears of the many — sheepish couples hid in the date forest. Apollo uses stenos. Poseidon wheezes, in his fenced villa, that leans as seas bellow. Youths pine, hid in the furnace, guarded beneath remote gazes, long breeze-arabesques, wafts of being fanning the age with myth's resin. Now, zed tanks, in situ, are boiling at their own speed in Gehenna's pitch, while Putin fills his corpse sack.

37. A Waft of Ether

When mercury adulterates the wake
of the last vaporetto, at the end
of Sant' Elena, the moon—trepanned,
his bare skull glowing with electroshock—

wanders the antiseptic corridors
of an abandoned hospital (the doctors left
their starched white coats, their charts, a drowsy waft
of ether); sallow, face a mess of sores,

sometimes he thinks he is Napoleon,
sometimes Attila or the Son of God,
a blind Doge heading up a Christian horde,
a doubled beast on Noah's galleon...

He drags his bathrobe sash across the tiles
of drizzly squares like empty shower stalls,
left on by other shaved and numbered souls,
stone faces broken by archaic smiles.

Drowsy Mercury wanders corridors of broken faces; doubled in God's sores or hospital tiles, he — blind, empty, his stone-white bathrobe on — awake at last as Christ. Their numbered smiles and souls of drizzly ether, abandoned by a moon glowing like a skull, their astral etude heading up the charts... the Son drags a cross by shallow doctors of the Other. The beast, a starched horde of coats, left an antiseptic waft. He stalls sometimes. The end of the archaic show, is the shock of His face — when Napoleon and Attila repent, saved. Not the mess of ash time's gales left. Here, on some bare square or on a vaporetto, elect gods think and heal with sane elan.

38. Santa Maria Nova

Today the sky is concrete and distressed:
Gribaudo's painting of a cardinal
facing away. Droplets begin to fall
like clear, pneumatic spirits bored of rest,

identical but for the splash they make.
The pitted matrix bulges where the roots
of broad trees crack their knuckles, or new shoots
of unsubdued *viriditas* retake

the stony field of Santa Maria Nova.
A well-dressed elder sits, bestowing roles:
like dissipated counts in dirty stoles,
the ruffled pigeons bow and wander over.

The church, lavish inside, is balneal
with fractured tiles and yellowed porcelain.
At night the lustrous grey unveils again
the smudged bazaar of the imaginal.

With like and like to spirit away the dissipated concrete, pneumatics crack their knuckles at night's bazaar. Us pigeons wander the fractured bog-porcelain sky. The count's smudged broad is bored, sits for a new painting. Dirty, tepid droplets splash where a stony field bulges. Cardinal shoots retake the roots of grey of elder Dis. The church of Santa is overt and arid. Yellowed but ruffled, balneal tiles in Maria of the Trees, they beg again the role the Fall stole. Make well today; bow, facing the nova, lavish-tressed matrix dressed in viriditas: identical bestowing of the lustrous imaginal, unveils rest, unsubdued and clear inside.

39. Patron of Corners

Walking in Cannaregio, one sooner
or later comes upon Her shabby state —
beside the bank, whose name one might translate:
mercy's foundation — facing Sullaluna

(the cafe also selling children's books),
where meeting walls of many strata shield
a hidden playground and a sporting field,
and tufts of green peek through the ruddy bricks:

patron of corners, breasting smaragdine
canals that stitch together without seam,
holding an infant Who has lost an arm,
above foundations blackened by the brine,

under a canopy of mouldy ply-
wood raised as if upon a music stand.
She holds against the wind, with weathered hand,
the old star-eaten blanket of the sky.

Lost star, raised out of old green brine, together with many mouldy, fust-blackened books. She has a weathered name Who, sporting Her smaragdine shield against the same blank aulas, walking through shabby walls, facing a hidden sky, translates that one-field-state, sooner or later rent. Mercy's the foundation of foundations, beside canals of meeting—holding the Infant, under and above the play of play and ground, a Child the might of Whose arm holds an arcing aeon by hand. Bank where wind-music comes. One apart, eaten, upon wood faces the total ruddy itch's null bare sting within. Any poet can stand upon bricks on corners, keep selling the *as if* star.

40. The Naked Masts

In uttermost Castello, costumes fray
to scraps of streamers, fading washing pinned
on lines like prayer flags in an empty wind.
The naked masts at the marina sway.

Policemen, with their riot-masks removed,
pace through the park; beside the football pitch,
a whippet shivers, covering a bitch
glossy, well-fed and visibly unmoved.

On Via Garibaldi acrid smoke
blankets a stage where children's songs are sung.
A distant tree looks like a blackened lung.
The city wheezes desperately, as if it woke

just before dawn, and — struggling to breathe —
in granular, forsaken half-light sees,
through curtains like a web of rosaries,
dawn blood the thorns in merciless reprieve.

A distant dawn; fading smoke covering the glossy and forsaken city, where merciless policemen, struggling with a riot of masks, desperately unmoved, sway in their blackened costumes like flags an acrid wind frays to scraps. Well-fed web streamers bitch and brag, as in the Iliad. Set before blank stage curtains, lungs like masts, like lace, shiver beside the empty, granular, just-woken marina. Pets on lines pace a ballpark. Arise Rosa, visibly removed; reprieve lost looks, through prayers a naked dawn wheezes, half-sung through the blood. At the uttermost pitch on the tree of song, an I afire pined to see Light breathe in its children via: foot-washing, whip, thorns.

41. Between These Shores

The dead are sleeping soundly, just across
the dark canal, their reading lights turned off;
at 3am, you might hear someone cough
or drily snore beneath their quilt of moss.

But, at this hour, silence walks their shelves,
patiently sorting through her growing pile
of airport lives — methodic, aisle by aisle,
like a librarian replacing selves.

On this side, there are people still awake,
sitting in cafes, drinking Aperol,
as in a tidy park, before a stroll
beside a leaf-strewn ornamental lake.

Between these shores the vaporetti roam —
coast guards patrolling boats of refugees
escaping silently through cypress trees
towards a skyline carved from styrofoam.

But by eating it die, to be like Someone that lives silently in you, awake early, before this dark canal dead refugees are strewn across, from their carved-leaf boats. Stroll still, reading between shores, escaping a peeling skyline. This hour of the ornamental cypress, walks patiently through a park, a pile of silence growing on moss — beneath patrolling lights — methodic as trees. Airport people sit replacing selves. Hear a guard cough in wards, a librarian roam sorting shelves. 3am vapor. Drinking the tidy lake. Cafes just *there*, turned off. Styrofoam drily quilts their coast. At Her rosen side, might their parole sound across these rote isles of aisles?

42. Distinguished Graves

There is, here, no periphery that bleeds
into the concrete real of tower blocks;
here, the circumference of rusted clocks
fades like a marsh-bank into mist and reeds.

Only the common dead enjoy a raw
and brutalist utility; they rest,
of all but honest ashes dispossessed,
in cells that bare their photo on the door.

Even in death they are consigned to live
in neat and comfortable synonymy.
Nearby, pointe shoes, left by some votary
wilt, pink, upon the tomb of Diaghilev.

The bora strums Stravinsky's empty staves;
the brittle ideogram of E. P.'s bones
rattles, as Brodsky rhythmically intones,
and time is lavished on distinguished graves.

The marsh's raw ideograms. The votary, in mist rusted, fades into a photo of that distinguished brutalist death: bare, brittle sand towers of utility; upon some comfortable, even blocks—concrete graves of synonymy—honest ashes lavished in common. The dead, dispossessed of real time, by the circumference of neat clocks (that bora strums reeds on a bank) they wilt, bleed into shoes of bone, point and rattle their staves; nearby, the periphery rhythmically intones. Brodsky, Stravinsky, Diaghilev, and E. P.—consigned to the tomb. But the only door is here, in all empty, pink cells. They Is as One: rest live and enjoy. Here, there are no likes left.

43. The Island of the Dead

You sail out to the island of the dead,
so like the Böcklin in your grandma's flat.
St Michael waits to weigh outstanding debt
upon the balance of a rusted blade;

the mist is lotion for the verdigris
that flakes from him in wafers of decline.
The vaporetto carves a serpentine
cortege; the cypresses are forgeries

so perfect even jaded connoisseurs
of symbolism miss the difference.
The dead line up behind the barbed-wire fence
of withered roses; customs officers

ransack their steamer trunks for contraband;
herded with others, Pound and Brodsky pass
below deck — poets travel second class —
each with a biro number on his hand.

So the dead, like withered connoisseurs, ransack and weigh flakes of grandma's symbolism, to fence for a pound. Flat island of balance. Even outstanding trunks of cypresses are in decline. Behind the forgeries — number upon mist. Jaded officers sail, with the contraband of difference below deck. Poets miss the rusted vaporetto, travel on a steamer, pass up the alchemic lotion for the verdigris sky, brood with Him dead, each biro line a barbed-wire cortege to others. Debt St is serpentine, outwaits the customs of the herded class, their second-hand wafers. His blade carves perfect roses from your . . . blink.

44. A Taxonomy of Fates

An installation on San Servolo,
composed of perforated oval plates
of metal. A taxonomy of fates,
freed from oblivion's faded calico;

photos of inmates from the hospital:
women, most young, some vacant, eyelids closed
or with the eyes of a Blavatsky, posed
by hidden doctors; with a peasant shawl

wrapped round her head, a finger on her lip,
another seems immersed in some new thought
in which she will remain forever caught —
punctured by needles, like a comic strip

divided into atoms, small black dots
which try to coalesce into a face.
A hotel and resort complex replace
the wards of women tethered to their cots.

Caught on photos (of a hotel, of another resort) oblivion's black atoms strip to their will, which posed women of San Servolo, in palest calico, punctured with needles like a metal finger, by some doctors of a cosmic hospital ward. Eyes closed or vacant on a young head, try to remain immersed in the round thought of fate. She freed tethered inmates from a lab vat, from eyelids' faded taxonomy, by which the sky seems divided. Women, wrapped in Her peasant shawl, composed Her an installation: cots coalesce to replace a perforated oval, lips, some dots, with a forever new and complex small face of the Most Hidden.

45. The Mooring Lines

Two old men, guarded by a threadbare mutt,
are sorting cockles into plastic tubs,
and drying out their traps and fraying webs.
The doors of St Euphemia are shut;

you search the flaking greenery for cracks.
Shaded by scarred facades, the promenade
is hosed-down like a migrant's concrete yard.
Like vintage postcards on revolving racks,

the shopfronts are hand-colorised; you start
to see in one a tan C64—
its old magnetic tapes now only store
side-scrolling memories of pixel art.

A civic centre shows the generation
of 68, released from photo archives.
A careful deckhand uses leather gloves
to coil the mooring lines until they groan.

Shaded generation of facades, mooring by a concrete Styx promenade — flaking memories on the guarded archive's leather doors — until the one magnetic centre cracks in two. *To see*, seeled, searches for a clock hand. Like webs to trap *the they*, a plastic art fraying into pixel shopfronts, scrolling greenery, the tape's *side a* revolving... and now you are shut out. Released from their racks and hosed down, the scarred men of Euphemia St only groan. In threadbare civic gloves, cold righteous fixity shows, sorting migrants by hand like vintage postcards.

46. Sepia Pawnshop

Wet sheets are wind-struck, as a pea-soup storm
batters the cafe awnings at the shore.
A sodden football pitch emits a roar
behind grey walls. The waiter's uniform —

as he folds chairs, a guttering cigar
between his lips — is like a seagull left
on some low mudbank, shivering, bereft,
overexposed by flashing camera.

The ripping water is a dirty mint;
alluvial deposits coalesce
from calligraphic voids of fogginess
into this sepia pawnshop for the skint,

who have only their memories to hock.
The calli smell of turps, from studios
where painters render objects otiose —
as, every hour, other artists dock.

Artists guttering into flashing sepia fogginess. Shivering painters render the hour of over-exposed objects; their studio walls are like wet water. Every camera is left on. Low chairs at a dock cafe as emits football. Some, ripping a sodden uniform, have to coalesce between mint sheets, as skin, the alluvial mudbank roar. By this bereft shore: a fort, a pawn, the only sea-gull hops. A waiter's grey lips, calligraphic cigar. Turps smell from His otiose other. Behind storm folds, where He Who Is batters wind-struck memories. From dirt, an ape posits the I opus, hocks the call of wings. The void's pith decays.

47. A Faded Driftwood Chair

Lido is better on a bicycle;
the placid, residential streets unroll
like thoughtless photos as you swipe and scroll;
you flow past, breezy, lackadaisical.

Both the Des Bains and the Excelsior
are closed for renovations. Thomas Mann
dozes at seaside, in a linen sun,
reclining in a faded, driftwood chair.

In Malamocco walls are mangled smooth;
they steam between the rolls of sand and sea.
It's always Sunday, but last century.
Until enlightened bureaucrats approve

the plans—inside some filing cabinet
deep in a musty basement where the rats
work double shifts like junior bureaucrats—
the hospital rots in a spider's net.

In Malamocco, a Sunday band plans dozens of seaside residential renovations. Lido abides as abient and null steam, its alkali scrolls roll, botch the star better. Some placid junior Thomas (the bureaucrat's bureaucrat) reclining in a driftwood chair, approves filing you, mangled work Man, in a deep basement you closed on the inside, where a smooth thoughtless double like a faded photo (sea swipe in sand) is, and the past's misty linen rots. But the core lexis always flows breezy between hospital walls; they are enlightened in shifts, for century or cycle in the spider's net streets, until at last cicadas are like the sun.

48. Pellestrina

You take the ferry, with your hired bike,
having already ridden down the Lido.
Flotsam, thrown together by tornado,
forms fishing sheds on this side of the dike,

conjoined with twins in laxly burnished pewter:
ramshackle colonies of rusted metals,
on hairy stilts and with a skirt of cockles.
A sparse, mixed-grill on a ceramic platter,

at *da Celeste*, as a brick-red barge
creases the foil, with digger figurehead.
Some distant, excavated storm clouds shed
muted electrum on a dented targe.

Returning, you must charge a windmill, blue
with cold, as wind sandblasts the straining boats—
an angry child at play with coloured floats—
and tears the flaxen pennants of bamboo.

The Child at play, having torn down cold clocks, sheds the distant blue figurehead, an angry idol of rusted metal, later excavated, burnished by colonies of bees, returning on clouds, with the elect conjoined with a foil — with the muted, hairy, rage-ridden herd. Straining pewter blasts a dented ferry, rigged fishing boats. Storm with electrum stabs. Ramshackle bamboo pennants tilt as wind creases your flaxen skirt. You and I, flotsam already thrown on this side, shed sparse tears together, as coloured floats — twins of forms — adapt the wind's charge (*Dikē* mixed with sand), rage laxly on and on at a like-mill of red brick. Some Adamic core within you must take the Grail.

49. Needle Lace

You see Torcello's russet wastes across
the channel, sparse with stubborn mangrove shrubs;
a wind in white gloves delicately rubs
the sky with solvent on a cloth of moss.

An Ithaca of brightly painted stone:
Penelope makes needle-lace from hairs
gone white in waiting for the splash of oars.
The horde, abandoning Attila's throne,

bear pillaged gold and flashing candelabra,
placards or flags taped to police batons,
as they begin the pilgrimage of clones,
fading beyond a heavy-laden arbor.

You hear the click of moulting crabs at work:
rebuilding husks of churches—citadels
on sucking mud—out of discarded shells,
to gleam pearlescent through polluted murk.

Insolvent throne of Ithaca. Penelope's arbor laden with moss. Crabs hear the click of white gloves, across flashing stone waste or atlas. See: flags of churches; a horde of police rub gleaming batons, they channel the king of clones; Carson's placards — taped on oars delicately discarded in hell's polluted mud make a sparse splash. Stubborn moulting husks abandon wind, pilgrimage forgone, to work at heavy needle, pillaged gold rebuilding the Sun's fading cloth, beyond citadels of white lace. A pearlescent sky rubs its hair with ash from the painted grove. Through the russet murk of cellos, You, the Man bear candelabra brightly, to You, and to us waiting to begin.

50. High Prattle

Almost a dozen sonnets, lost in Rome.
When spring became too much for me I fled
the sunlit, fleshpot streets and visited
Keats; but, a couple sitting near the tomb,

entangled, shared a joint and filled the air
with their high prattle, smoke untouched by wind:
all *copy copies, all increase their kind.*
Motley cast down beside the marble stair

is all this phantom labour will deliver.
Postcards from Italy. *I think of cities*
Vicenza, Verona, Venice, clarities
enduring for a while beside some river...

On our first crossing, did I hesitate
as we unmoored, approached the other side?
In green scrubs, she unplugs whoever died.
The vessel hardly seemed to bear my weight.

But a copy, entangled, a prattle-filled flesh, sitting beside a green tomb in Rome, unmoored withal, I lug puns, labour down river, cast a smoke net for phantom marble clarities, lost sunlit streets, post-cards, their Italy — Vicenza, Verona, Venice . . . cities fled as motley copies of some other. While Keats scrubs the untouched enduring vessel. Spring approached me, She did, I think — is *seemed*. Too much wind. I hesitate, near the top stair, hardly bear my crossing, this joint air the dozen, side by side, shared. When will we increase forever, and the Most-High — Who became our kind, and died to deliver all from the weight the first couple visited on their sons — be all in all?

PART TWO

> ...memory too is an idea: you think
> rationally but you feel your thoughts,
> and watch them rise, Byzantine, in a square
> heavy with cupolas whose breasts are bare
> ideas of breasts that no idea supports,
> canals, black water, waking dreams, rough drink.
> —*George Szirtes*

> *I can see someone walking there, a girl,*
> And she is you, old love. Edging the meadow
> The may-tree is all light and all shadow.
> Coming and going are the things eternal.
> —*Geoffrey Hill*

> The furies are at home
> in the mirror; it is their address.
> Even the clearest water,
> if deep enough can drown.
> —*R. S. Thomas*

51. The Garish Show

A long way down the lamp-lit shore of slaves —
a Christmas funfair on the dark canal:
a marksman hunts a fluffy animal,
the thump of dodgems drowns the lisping waves.

Although the sky is clear, frenetic stars
obscure their heavenly originals.
The games of chance on offer at the stalls
promise one endless foam-filled avatars.

The tinny midi music of arcades —
where childhood spent its pocket money — plays,
and carousels revolving in a daze
of light and laughter that returns and fades

bring centaurs round, again, in miniature.
The coloured balls that hot-air from below
keeps tumbling to preserve the garish show
will rise or fall, of that one can be sure.

Although: dark laughter hunts slaves in the frenetic lamp-lit daze of the Fall's miniature arcades, a tinny man on the dodge pockets sure money of marks spent on fun games, hot coloured balls revolving keep the sombre show on its way, a chance canal drowns the obscure originals tumbling from one clear sky down along a shore of garish foam that fluffy waves thump at—the endless round of avatars bring and offer stars that fade to the Christmas stall below, where the heavenly childhood plays. Fair music. Lips sing, in a care of souls that can and will preserve the promise of their dim I's return and rise. The recusant animal is again light-filled air.

52. The Ramifying Narrative

The Riva here is empty. You begin
(near coloured lights above a cafe door
that leads both *in*—onto the sawdust floor—
and *out* the circus dome beneath the skin)

anew the ramifying narrative:
stray conversations in the dialects
of ruined textures, books of plaster sects;
seeing light trace a shadowed pendentive;

avoiding pigeons grey as refugees
who mill, hunch-shouldered, in internment camps
beneath stone towers with their flashing lamps;
the midnight bells of tourists fumbling keys;

a water rat whose wake unstitched a seam
of satin lining, deep within the folds
of sober black. The ancient truce still holds,
among the frontline trenches of a dream.

A ruined light towers, flashing anew among ramifying conversations: tourists, dialects, stray leads, deep folds of lining unstitched. The dream, shouldered, beneath a shadowed narrative (the satin internment-dome of the Ancient of Grey above, who holds the keys to a stone circus, whose hunched black lamps wake and trace the camps). Within mill sober refugees, frontline sects in their plaster, fumbling the saw-dust. In both — still textures — you, avoiding the empty midnight without door, here near the seam of seeing, coloured trenches of light's truce at the skin, as thin bells of water, pendent, begin. A Riva cafe: pigeons, books, beneath — on the floor — a rat.

53. City of Misdirection

Above the smokestacks: sombre rose, swept gulls.
The hotel Stucky looms in ruddy brick.
Furred eels of seaweed ripple in the swells
that tumble from Guidecca. Walking back

along Zattere, hands in pockets, cold
from having sat too long on wave-lapped walls,
you feel your bones like columns growing old,
and lose yourself in labyrinthine malls.

City of misdirection, silvered maze.
The mirrored corridors proliferate:
dark alleys dogleg into other days;
courtyards enclose denuded trees of fate.

Sottoportici of graffitied brick
lead to a monument for those who don't exist.
Grey nuns of order gently tend the sick.
Escheresque bridges founder in the mist.

The pocket-founder of the cold, silvered city of fate tends grey looms, above a too-sombre monument to order on alike columns of bones. Smoke swells and ripples from dark-red stacks. In your denuded hand: the sick, labyrinthine rose. Misdirection: mirrored in alleys misty eels proliferate. Stuck for days in the ruddy maze (Zattere, Guidecca, sottoportici, long seaweed-lapped malls...), the old wave-swept Hotel Escher's graffitied corridors gull you. In dog fur, walking back along other bridges — those gently led to courtyards that enclose nuns who don't exist feel trees growing. Lose yourself, in quest of *legein*; as the walls of having tumble brick from brick.

54. On the Margins

Two times you tried to get to Zattere
by vaporetto, near the Stucky mill
that still grinds golden grain inside its till.
Your phone is dead, an empty battery;

there is no way to call the concierge
at your hotel. The water taxis cost
so much this late it's better to be lost
in this unbidden cul-de-sac, diverge

from your intended journey to the real,
on the last vaporetto to depart
bound for the one Piazza. Set apart,
here, on the margins—near illegible

beside the text of cupolas and bars—
you try to read the faintly pencilled notes
the moon imparts to student hermeneuts,
where boys catch *seppie* under yellow stars.

On your intended journey depart, O student. The cost: to be lost in force, the times' faintly illegible taxis, to catch unbidden moon-text pencilled on the water, by your call, dead stars, you golden grain. Not one set apart, the Real sows to impart — this last piazza, its much tried cupolas and you beside. From the sepia pen, the concierge of margins grinds Hermes' tune, the notes still inside, till the two — vaporetto under vaporetto — diverge. Where, bound to the phone, the empty ulcerated boys mill near bars, yell Z, get better at battery, its late. Near hotel Stucky, try to read your way: this is to that as here is to there.

55. Other Portals Wait

The Calle dei Marrani can convey
the wanderer into another world;
much like the first, just ominously veiled—
like those tense scenes in *Stalker*, where they play

an eerie game of warehouse hide-and-seek
with a policeman. Other portals wait
to bend consensus: build another state,
whose sheer facades are flush and do not creak,

lit like a fish-tank in a shopping mall,
in which a shark is circling endlessly
nosing a trace of blood lost out at sea.
The entrance must be unintentional:

become the part and cock your sailor's hat—
linger at windows full of kitsch, embossed
volumes—take corners as if really lost,
stumble into a frame by Hugo Pratt.

If those volumes of blood be lost at the mall, whose are they, policeman? Eerie kitsch become unintentional consensus, shopping facades endlessly frame the entrance to the world warehouse: full windows lit like portals, scenes of tank and cock. Sailors, circling a flush, lost, wander a sea which first rain must mar, sheer and embossed. Linger, build another trace to the Other. A tense shark, ominously at play with another take, I stumble like a Stalker in a hat, nosing just by a sere bend, where the veiled really do hide, and cannot convey much. Die in part, wait out the game of state, in an ought trap; it creaks like a scorner. Seek your call.

56. Veritas

The Rio Terà dei Pensieri ends
with a long prison wall and leafless trees
that guard the pigeons' leaden reveries.
The path to water leads through stony fronds;

the craft enjambs its flow with practiced glide—
a worker in fluorescent weather gear
and waders at the helm; the name is clear
upon the barge and just above the tide,

in glossy letters painted: *Veritas*.
It docks awhile, bisected by a bridge
of coarse red brick; I'm watching at the edge
of a jade rio, as the barges pass.

This one is hoovering the past day's shit—
it revs its epistemic engine, green
as hope—by means of hose that, serpentine,
digests an elephant, becomes a hat.

Day's painted, brick-red barge docks, just as it is, at the edge of the epistemic; by means of it one clear flow is bisected, as water becomes name. Serpentine letters bridge the long green past; upon its glossy path jade barges pass. In waders, hope leads the stony worker through a coarse tide that laps and digests rio by rio. I'm with the pigeons that glide over the fronds and trees. A practiced craft enjambs the shithose awhile. The veritas-engine above revs in gear. Guard a leaden tear of leafless reveries: prison weather, hate and hating. *To die* ends; watching the fluorescent station wall, the I repines. Aha!—Athene with a helm.

57. Games of Chance

The only cafe open on the mall
lends you a lighter. Inside, people dance
like beads inside a beer glass. Games of chance
with flashing buttons, and the clocks are all

turned to the wall in dunce hats. Power drills
displayed in lights inside a hardware store,
like zoo-bound predators too bored to roar
at gawkers tapping at the glass for thrills.

The ground is strewn with garish alphabets
the coloured-paper symbols babble; stirred,
by winds that stumble home, they form a word—
a flash-mob, each one instantly regrets.

The awning automatically retracts
at midnight and the broken chairs are led
back to their stable. Homeless echoes bed
down under blankets of the latest facts.

The roar of bored facts, stirred by power. The Word, in each bound, broken form, led to stumble under the ground's echoes and regrets. A mob babble. Garish thrills are automatically strewn for gawkers with their hats and beer, at the latest midnight. The homeless glass, inside the stable people inside you: symbols, displayed on a wall like coloured lights at the mall cafe. Predators, too at home inside the alphabet zoo, flashing hardware, tapping game buttons, send based likes. All a rill-bed stored is instantly turned; the one wind dances with *Charis*, to steer the lot. A lighter dawning, in nuce, opens paper tracts. Blank chance backs down, clocks the flash of that only glass They are.

58. The Veil Itself

Silence falls on the avenue of lamps,
softer than mist, softer than silence — twin
to its apparent self; when words begin
filling the album with the rarest stamps,

the memory of it is like the pale
paper between the regimented rows,
semi-transparent, through which dimly glows
the commerce of the world as through a veil.

The veil itself, however filmy, sheer
as the sheerest silk, is still a wall
immeasurably thin, the liminal
and hazy clarity where things appear.

It is as if you saw yourself beyond
a lit-up window, watching yourself write,
hunched on a bench beneath the haloed light,
as soundless instants drip into a pond.

Sheerest silence, immeasurably still, stamps world into haloed mist of memory, filling the hunched words between with a twin silence, dimly beyond itself, when the apparent falls beneath the filmy pond, as regimented instants of a thin sheer self — like pale paper lamps, through which it glows transparent — and semi-things appear on the wall. The rarest veil is watching yourself begin to write. Liminal commerce: how, through the album-window, you saw the hazy avenue where your self rows a bench, on the softer-than-silk veil of the *as if*—as ever, softer than clarity; its soundless light drips, as the *it* is lit up: a the is *a the*.

59. The Poem Bleeds

Someone is flying kites with EU stars.
Old irredentists doze in public parks.
A kneeling worker showers golden sparks,
grinding the grid of flattened metal bars

protecting the post office from a run
on express envelopes... It could be worse.
The last coin falls into a beggar's purse.
The world will end sometime this afternoon —

just as you hear a name you'd soon forget,
or clean a leaking fountain pen of ink;
or as a waitress smiles, too tired to think
and half-way through her *final* cigarette.

No time to buy a sky-blue writing pad;
a napkin is sufficient for your needs,
though too absorbent, so the poem bleeds
too much for what you've written to be read.

A beggar's cigarette falls through a grinding sky, showers sparks as though from time's end. A waitress's half-smile. Golden fountain of the Name. Just irredentists kneeling for the last world. Flying a clean napkin kite, in your old sufficient public park, sometimes you'd forget the final poem, our tune, is written this way. Tired ink-worker, you've read: the star to be bleeds. Her protecting blue envelopes a flattened afternoon. As a someone — leaking needs in pad, office, or bar — is writing on the absorbent *could be* no *what* pens with a grid. Too, too, too much to hear and so express, and soon you will buy it or worse — doze to think for a purse of post-metal coin.

60. Black Dog

Beside the streetlight is a red park bench.
A man walks past it with a stout black dog.
Sometimes the street lamp wraps herself in fog
as if in ermine; she abhors the stench

that, at high tide, will rise from pipes and drains
like a conspiracy. Spotlights of hard
awareness punctuate the promenade.
Sometimes a rat scrapes gravel, or it rains,

or someone standing at a window hears
the dusty battering of moths beyond
the glassy surface of a midnight pond.
On that red bench, once every dozen years,

an old man sits and lights a cigarette.
A statue lifts a bottle to stay warm
and huddles shivering inside its form.
At dawn the lamp goes out, the bench is wet.

A wet-dog-stench huddles. Black rain, battering at a statue inside the streetlight, is a dusty conspiracy of moths. A dozen pipes drain the promenade tide of form and red light. A rat abhors street lamps, scrapes at every window. Or, sometimes, if fog She wraps herself in lifts, the past—a stout man a warm bottle lit—sits on a hard bench the bench spotlights, beside an old pond with its bench that goes to stay. Or, sometimes, the glassy dawn awareness *is*—beyond the high years shivering in ermine—will surface from someone, standing like a lamp, as red cigarettes punctuate the midnight park. At once, the man that hears it rises out of a grave and walks and...

61. The House of Craftsmanship

Taming the wood to fit the skeleton,
men caulk between the lines with fragrant pitch;
feasting at midday on a lustrous catch,
beneath the ribcage of Leviathan,

they work to build another floating trope.
The bakers knead hard tack from ash and foam.
A mermaid wrestles tangles with a comb
of bone and plaits her tresses into rope.

On massive harps, old women weave the cloth,
sow canvas in the house of craftsmanship.
Nearby, with laughter, vagrant children skip
a chalky outline on a sunlit path.

Divided labour hums, as chisels pray
preparing cross-beams for another mast
that wind might swell the fabric of the past —
they can rebuild the city in a day.

Nearby, the hard past chisels a sermon, preparing another cross. Women and men pray, divided as a harp, a comb for lustrous tresses; they weave plaits from trope tangles, to rebuild the day's fabric; they sow on foam: build, work beams of wood, pitch cloth to fit that ship mast, craft lines that can rope the fragrant wind. Beneath a massive floating ribcage — the might of a sunlit vagrant taming the naked skeleton at midday — feasting and laughter swell in the city of ash. Break the caul. Skip, with a nack, the path between a chalky bone, to catch another Man's outline. The Maid wrestles in labour with Her children. On old canvas, the house of Levi hums with kin.

62. Spices from Acre

Far from the hidden courts where dyers soak,
in vats of squid-ink, the Republic's sails,
resisting windows of Murano grails,
you run the gauntlet of a neon souk.

Men unload endless barges at the wharves.
Beneath the arches fish are multiplied.
Sandstorms of scent enfold the stalls of dried
spices from Acre. Ships bring: Tartar slaves

from Tana, pirates from Dalmatian coves,
captured in raids by floating caravans.
Pale, noble women buy gold-handled fans.
In alcoves, statues beg for scattered loaves.

Near bottles labelled *Aphrodite's Foam*,
an object-forger reasons with a buyer.
Searching deep pockets for loose change, you hire
a stooped *codega* to escort you home.

These men are Adam, beg far from home, in Latin mourning: sandstorms of a pale gold scattered where change stalls in an acre of neon, bottles of dried republics for hire. The object pirates run the slave coves. Noble fans buy escort women from a forger, stooped by the gauntlet of spice caravans. Aphrodite's statues soak in the tan vats, multiplied at endless windows. You enfold sails, resisting the raids of foam — reason's scent, a code hidden from you beneath the dyer's tar. For you, ships unload loaves from loose pockets, near rat-captured wharves; barges bring labelled grails to a buyer. Fish search the deep souk courts, squid-handled alcoves, arches, sagas floating in ink.

63. Mute Industry

Beside a window, needle paused at poise,
she holds some fine, discrete embroidery;
weighed in the balance of fidelity:
mute, inner industry and worldly noise.

It's noon; the sun above — a shrill citrine,
a manic yellow, gambling to the last.
The smell of failure lingers in the past
like must inside a second-class vitrine,

displaying objects too polite to speak:
her horse-tail switch, her styluses of bone.
In walnut painted to resemble stone,
her chest contains the plunder of the weak.

By manumission tempted to betray,
slaves may appropriate forbidden chests,
serve peacock to time's iridescent guests,
possess the pearls that they may not display.

Embroidery of the switch lingers. She, paused beside a walnut vitrine, tempted to speak above the shrill noise of her guests, slaves to resemble some fine painted window, displaying the bone chest inside her chest that contains time's discrete pearls the weak may hold not possess. It's appropriate. They must serve mute objects to the last second: the manic gambling of worldly industry, forbidden failure, past inner poise like stone horses, too weighed in the balance by the sun's manumission — the citrine-yellow styluses of May and iridescent peacock tail of plunder — to betray the polite smell of class. A needle displays her infidelity.

64. The Palette of Diminished Greens

He sweeps the calle with a stiff, wet broom;
a disinfectant angel is invoked.
The cobbles yield—where fiery bristles stroked—
in whispers all the flotsam of their doom.

The now is chemical; it burns and cleans
(the city, lifted like a fingerprint
out of its body into what it meant,
completes the palette of diminished greens);

it is the clarity in which they fade
into themselves, renouncing what they show.
A blush betrays this motionless tableaux.
A figure pauses in the enfilade

of light intended. Daphne promptly leaves—
down all the detours crackling like noise,
spreading like 7000 oaks that Beuys
planted in Kassel. Then, Apollo grieves.

The motionless all out of themselves complete their intended figure. Renouncing the light of now, in clarity, diminished in the body, He sweeps down. The angel that betrays is lifted. They grieve doom, in the city of whispers and wet green cobbles, where leaves fade like noise-slaked pauses, fade like the Nile. Promptly they soak 7000 planted stiffs. A broom bristles. Disinfectant cleans the chemical tableaux. Apollo strokes Daphne's fingerprint, yields to detours like the meant by use. In a blush of flotsam—the *what*, invoked in a call, spreading its fiery palette, with which this crackling show burns what is into all: as *it* then *I*. I eat it.

65. Foundation Mists

At dawn, the sweepers with their witch's brooms
appear to drive confetti, ticket stubs
and cigarettes, dressed in their civic scrubs
like orderlies in ether-scented rooms.

At last, like patient archaeologists —
who with soft brushes would unearth the past —
their scrapes will free the city from its cast
of fact, revealing its foundation-mists.

While dentists grind the plaque patina down
to find the tooth beneath discoloured smiles,
they scrape the marble from the caried piles,
see past the lion's grin (the golden crown

of the Piazza capped in common lead),
in league with pigeons, waves and mousy rain
that swarms the gutters of the rich demesne
time's meek, grey children have inherited.

The sweeper's league, in scraps with the stinted city, drive their brooms (while they wave their cigarettes at past scented confetti), win the piazza, from fact-orderlies in mousy scrubs with ether-mists, who would shave and geld the lion that stubs its marble tooth on gutters. See, time's mess-piles, the past scraped to escape. Find the ticket to the Civic Archaeologists' Foundation rooms, with Eden's plaque. Beneath the soft lead-grey patina of pigeon-like swarms, dawn brushes unearth rain discoloured smiles. At last, the patient, downcast, meek, free the common will from its inherited itch and grind—appear like children, dressed in their crowns, revealing the caried grin of the rich fop.

66. The Garbage Men

The garbage men, with massive shopping carts
they push before them, grim as Sisyphus,
until they reach the barge that lifts the mess
of refuse onboard with a crane that starts

to rumble like the rapture. All those pale,
blue plastic shades; the men in lurid, bright
waterproof outfits that reflect the light.
But then, instead, the boat is steered to sail

upstream of Lethe, like a salmon: blind
intent to reach the highland spawning grounds,
that drives the mailed stars upon their rounds.
For now, the wasted remnant of the mind

will lie on some low midden—grasping mud
chaining their feet, where memory and bliss
mingle like waters scaled and sinuous,
and couple—there to chew their bitter cud.

Blind, wasted shades reflect a memory of that upstream couple, in the blue bliss, the Now, before the reach of the sinuous lie chaining their grasping minds to proof, a pale remnant, and grounds like mud, where bitter boatmen—that drives led there—intent to rumble, chew their plastic mess, as the crane outfits them. Then, steered, they sail onboard their lurid garbage barge, until they reach the massive crud-midden upon Lethe, spawning the grim will to refuse the stars that mingle on low scaled water. And Sisyphus, on feet like those, starts to push the shopping cart. For some, pure art sounds like that. But, the highland water, the bright I AM, with alms of light is with and lifts all men.

67. Discreet Amanuensis

The theatre passage leads to Casa Polo
above the tunnel of a million things,
a capped well fed by subterranean springs.
Explorers, steaming up the river Yolo,

their craft heavy with plunder—in the reeds,
the current mingling blood and river-clay,
where they have docked to bargain or parley,
exchanging vistas for a string of beads.

Vaporous images: the hidden fleet,
sleek galleys prowling the Dalmatian coast;
Andrea Dandolo lashed to a mast,
cracking his skull in penance for defeat;

somnambulistic soirees, on and on...
he spills—for his discreet amanuensis,
a scribbler of Arthurian Romances—
from his slit lining: jewels and bullion.

The null boils. They have docked upon ash cay or lashed coast, where reeds well and a sleek river spills gain. You, this heir of His, scribble for *La Donna*, hidden and adored, exchanging the current defeat for vaporous Arthurian vistas. The blood, prowling a discreet subterranean passage, to plunder His jewels from clay. Penance, a string of a million beads, leads a fleet river to the springs of images above. Anamnesis in the skull theatre. Fed on romance, pale master-explorers, in the lining of things craft streaming somnambulistic galleys, mingling Dali with the Atman. Polo, caped, flits to soiree and bar, by cracking tunnel and heavy door.

68. A Bright Panache

A musky extract varnishing the boards.
Oppressive, scentless light insinuates:
the perfumed gloom of foreign consulates,
the bloodied crosses of Crusader swords,

the siege of tourists militantly gauche.
The pedestal removed, the stories stand;
incense supports a church in Samarkand.
The girl in veils, the head upon the dish,

the stars misfiled in fading microfiche,
the Silk Road washed away by desert tides.
Only the trade in images abides,
the soldier's helmet with a bright panache.

The truth is dark around the golden ore.
The only time that Marco Polo lied
was claiming to return; unoccupied
rooms are a bustling fair of metaphor.

The church militantly crosses the golden desert of truth; the soldiers, swords of oppressive light, bright helmets upon fair heads, return bloodied by the fading trade road. The siege, claiming the dark perfumed girl in the veils of metaphor, in the incense of scentless images the unoccupied pedestal supports, abides only in bustling chimeric stories that lie with panache of a silk gloom varnishing the stars. Time's foreign tide washed away St Marco. The drama sank in a pool. The musky, gauche crusader tourists stand around the consulate room, insinuate the broad's a dish. Was the arch-text, the I-seed, removed, or only misfiled, Erato?

69. The Masons of the Nameless Hand

The pilgrims puzzle over blue-and-taupe
projections of the labyrinth of chance;
like motes in motion, they perform their dance—
free play beneath a glassy microscope.

The huddled pigeons thrive on scattered crumbs;
like children at the seashore dripping sand—
their guild: The Masons of the Nameless Hand—
they build a Gaudi church to house the tombs.

It is unfinished still, but it will rise
again before the end, they are convinced.
This drawing room (immoderately chintzed),
by the corrosive coral of the skies

encrusted, will in times to come regain
its proper pallor: shades of graphite, tin
and ashes, shadowed by a baldachin
of wings that fade beneath the acid rain.

Apes, convinced of their projections on the free skies. Pilgrims are huddled in tomb pallor, shadowed by a church of sand. They eat pigeon and perform in ashes beneath glassy wings that dance beneath the Nameless. Chance, immoderately dripping corrosive time, rains that acid will. The Masons of the Bald Chin build a chintzed puzzle-room, at their microscopes. But, over this is the Right Hand. The coral labyrinth will end, the crumbs of it it it . . . rise again. Guiled shades, still unfinished like a children's drawing, fade in scattered motion, before they regain the house of play. They come, like Gaudi, to shore up encrusted tomes, and to thrive by the proper blue of the sea.

70. A Nameless Epitaph

Beside a nameless Latin epitaph,
set in a wall where jasmine trumpets peal,
your shadow leaves you for another path;
in waxen silence footsteps press their seal.

You will not find again your other life.
Calypso holds you in her coral net.
Another man walks past you with your wife,
his sea-grey eyes unruffled by regret.

The gondolas, like sable thoroughbreds,
are stabled for the night and buck their reins.
The Doges sleepless on their stately beds,
St Mark's square spins with feathered weathervanes.

St Theodore stands fasting, till the moon
inclines to him a species of its host;
he thinks the end-times must be coming soon,
only another thousand years at most.

A coral silence. The unruffled sea. At night, a nameless weather spins its vanes. By the most sable path, you find gods in pieces within the Latin net. Dun wall a St marks. Where jasmine inclines for another, see St Calypso fasting. The moon reins stately, stabled years. Another man holds your thoroughbred wife, walks beside her past your square epitaph. Feathered Hosts, with their thousand eyes, their trumpets peal another coming. The sleepless shadows will soon stand again, leave their grey beds. Press back, in His footsteps till your only end; for, He thinks you like you must be. You are not other to Him, the Seal set on time's waxen regret, Logos and Door of Life.

71. Written on a Tamarind

He died during a storm, delirious
(a history of music no one read
consumed his youth), his expedition failed,
mourned by the pygmies of Herodotus.

It's hot and windless. We must pull the boat.
The Nile follows its unchanging course;
we are still sailing on towards the source;
water narcissi on the surface float

and tangle up our craft in reverie.
The Lion of Uele and St Mark,
laps at the surface of a limpid dark.
The guides, who claimed they hunted ivory,

were slavers. *It is hot, no trace of wind.*
*The river flo*ws, so changeless it seems still.
Those coming to Galuffi later will
find *Miani* written on a tamarind.

Windless, mourned water follows its course, the pull towards a dark will; so, it seems, flows a river, changeless; at its surface no craft laps. The ivory guides are still. We read Herodotus (history, the delirious tangle of our hot *no*) and, later in the gym admire a lunate trace of *ipse*. We of the source must float up the hot Nile, Miani. Reverie of one music, unchanging if fugal. St Mark and his wind-hunted lion sailing on a boat; they were on it during the storm. And the Youth who, coming, consumed His failed expedition, died to find those claimed by slavers? He is still written on the limpid surface of narcissi.

72. A Dive Bar Stage

Down open veins of ordinariness
that buzz with neon and intoxicants,
shop alcoves where a mannequin repents
have their own garish saints that deign to bless

the pilgrim pausing here along the way
to his dead end, where water punctuates
the trailing sea-silk of his former states.
Slowly, like candles lit for Tenebrae,

smart phones extinguish. Then, the pewter moon—
a dish still bloody, in a haze of veils
that part like clouds—phlegmatically reveals
a dive bar stage where ageing sea-gulls croon.

The vaporetti like stout tug-boats guide
vast ships of fog across the Grand Canal,
erase the Lido to a liminal
anticipation of the other side.

Here a former act repents of rot; the bare idol-like part, a pilgrim mannequin, trailing veils of neon silk and garish veins along a tenebrous canal. For the grand unageing saints taste the cup, extinguish in anticipation, bless then guide the vast dead across that open still sea, that reveals the bloody tug of the moon water erases slowly, phlegmatically. A fog-haze of ordinariness clouds a liminal stage, where pausing states have their own alcoves, where gulls deign to dive down to that other side of the sea, like his candlelit pewter dish, where boats, vaporetti, smart shop-ships, buzz like phones, with intoxicants — on the way to His end.

73. The Ruin of Your Form

Red lights come on, beside the building site.
Below, the city spreads her spider legs,
adjusts the tension of the strings and pegs
and plucks the web to make it resonate;

around her, forms hang twirling, silk-entwined.
In windows, faceless bodies flaunt their wares;
bouncers outside boutiques smoke fat cigars.
Lean, fur-clad women enter, having dined

(prying from mussel shells like coffin lids
salty, tumescent flowers of the sea).
When you descend, into that gallery
to mine the darkness, for what coal it yields —

tell then, my beauty, to the verminous
mouths that will devour you, kiss by kiss,
that I have kept the measure of all this:
the ruin of your form in every glass.

When the glass I that hangs on the crag flaunts its will, clad in fur the light's I's around Her yield to the outside, make the sea resonate, prying lean salty shells of beauty. Then the fat spider plucks strings for all. Women adjust wares in boutique windows. Building from cur bones your site beside the elm, to faceless darkness, that mine below measure, coffin of forms and every what. Go: descend by steps the bodies' gallery, silk-smoke twirling in ruin; enter the city of tumescent kiss-lids that devour flowers. Having dined (their web-entwined legs) my verminous mouths spread. Tell Her this: you have kept the form and tension of us, you kiss to come like red coal.

74. The Chained Blue Door

Beneath the flash of parasitic screens,
the muddy bed is rank with rusted springs,
old tires like unsuccessful safety rings
watched by the portholes of washing machines;

though shallow, it is dangerous to ford.
The chained blue door beneath a pointed arch —
where costumed pairs still pose, in early March,
like fashion models, numinously bored —

is reached by crossing at the second bridge.
Calle de Mezo doglegs — but avoid
the slug of dogshit. Like a Polaroid
the place develops to the very edge

as you arrive, to veil the empty page . . .
Move fast enough, between the closing drapes,
and find a stubborn crop of frosted grapes,
a red bird singing in a silver cage.

A dangerous, chained bird of veils, with a rank red crop, fashions this unsuccessful place: arid pool beneath the flash of numinous rings, the parasitic singing where stubborn models like costumed machines develop in pairs. Bored, I watched a slug arrive in the safety of March. Though the made-cage is rusted, reached by a second, silver door-screen is a frosted-blue bridge, at the edge, crossing the shallow, subtly-beige void. Ford it to find, between closing muddy drapes, the spring beneath the arch-page. Enough of the posed grapes, old likely hero-plots. Still the din, poet; fast, washing early; be empty; rest like Zoe moves, as God calls to very God and to you.

75. Sei Tornato

So, *sei tornato*, as the waiter says,
his t-shirt torn, braving the morning frost
(another moment, artfully embossed
upon the seamless surface of your days).

His words flow, warm, into the cast of air
like molten plaster, hover in suspense,
briefly refuse to harden into sense
until you choose a woven-plastic chair.

Above the rafts, the dusty gulls revolve;
the Stucky mill fades like a milky ghost.
A boat growls like a dog tied to a post,
as modes of mist proliferate and selve.

The pigeons try, persistent as a vice,
to scavenge chips. In winter sun, the crowd
sip Aperol and ruminate aloud.
Dawn's crisp attention melts like floating ice.

As the ghost-mill days revolve, refuse sense. The plaster of a winter torn, until a warm attention — briefly seamless — fades in frost-crisp modes. Molten suspense: scavenge the dusty surface of a moment, aloud, as pigeons choose — artfully. Words harden to rafts of floating ice. A dawn boat growls, braving the persistent mist. Milky morning. Gulls hover like chips above the vice-woven crowd. A waiter melts into his chair; his embossed t-shirt says *post-plastic*. Sip another Aperol and ruminate upon selves, like you, cast into the flow and stuck. *Sei tornato.* Like a dog tied to the sun, try to like the air, proliferate your say-so...

76. Flâneur

His ritual umbrella held aloft,
the guide is dogged by noble connoisseurs
and, further back: the Russian dolls in furs,
the English muffins dressed like Lara Croft

beneath the resurrected Campanile,
Bermuda shorts and beige safari-vests
of portly Western Orientalists—
the only party that can rally freely.

The groups collide—where once piranha flags
had fed, cloth minnows mingle in the sun—
until the white sheet of oblivion
has swept them up like fake designer bags.

You serve the law, flâneur, despite your spleen—
the categorical imperative,
as formal as this massive marble sieve,
to see the sights that simply must be seen.

Piranha connoisseurs of English, noble flâneurs swept up by the spleen ritual, marble dolls that scan far and must serve the categorical designer, his formal imperative that sieves oblivion — as sight and seen mingle, beneath the law of the alike, now's massive cloth Aristotle held — these bear the Nile mud further. Only You simply, freely guide, once Your Sun in the croft is back aloft. Groups party, white flags rally, despite the vast fake ruins, a lair where short, portly, dogged Western men camp, dressed in sin's beige fur, fed muffin, collide (the thesis is: the gab had/has to be like this), until the Lamb's lure sees them resurrected.

77. Atlantis Waiting

The peculation of swift-fingered tides
has pilfered daylight's lustrous commonwealth,
to fund imperial fireworks by stealth.
Consider these sidereal altitudes —

as inky fingers turn the hollow globe
they plot their pattern on the fugitive
blackboard of water. Deep in Plato's Cave,
the moon glows dull — a sunken astrolabe.

The trees of porphyry and serpentine,
the columns of San Marco, subsidised
by tides of plunder and the New Rome razed,
by changeless valence of Venetian coin.

Each dawn brings tribute on a tide of blood,
contracted beauty rolled in salty scrolls.
The perfect city floats on muddy shoals —
Atlantis waiting for another flood.

Consider the imperial columns of Atlantis, razed by changeless tides, their perfect plunder of the moon's wealth. Plato, Porphyry... deep, serpentine cave pilfered by the new plot, by stealth contracted, as these shoals of blood, sunken altitudes of each salty Rome, awaiting — on and on — the fugitive valence of dawn. Marco scrolls the fingered, hollow globe. Lustrous glows of swift water. Fire works. And peculation fingers the pattern for trees. *The They* has a fund of dull coin, a stale orb. Venetian tides rolled in; another sidereal tide, the inky flood, in turn brings tribute to daylight's common beauty.

78. A Perfumery of Moods

The carnival seems busier this year:
like an invasion from the slums of faerie
we lace the mist, near where Carabinieri
in steaming locker rooms adjust their gear.

All this ornate fragility... What hides
in larvae made of papier-mâché?
What model do the students form in clay?
This skittish crowd—on which desire rides

like an aristocrat through morning woods—
why is it roused by stars that dig like spurs?
Like great lords, sweating in barbaric furs
we stray through a perfumery of moods.

Meanwhile, the clapper of San Zaccaria
beats on dull metal like a hammer blow—
first thrusts the tongue within the furnace glow
of noon, then quenches it in nights of fear.

What barbaric clay form roused the aristocrat of fragility, that thrusts papier-mâché larvae in the furnace? The dull clapper of noon. An invasion of Carabinieri quenches the steaming, sweating slums. Lords in skittish, ornate lace blow through. Students of faerie hammer stars from their spurs. The great carnival where, near the woods, a model crowd beats on stray moods. This tongue we desire, it hides like morning. We adjust, made like; busier, glow on gear in locked rooms. Meanwhile, within — nights of fear or... what year is this? It seems the First rides by this perfumery of *why* in furs. Like then, in San Zaccaria. What a mist! Dig through the All: like like...

79. Shallow Recollections

A crane wades like a giant waterbird.
The vaporetti churn the milky jade,
only a few insomniacs on board
these all-night diners of the graveyard trade.

A winged lion roars inaudibly.
Three drunken tourists, wearing plastic masks,
too late for Carnival, drown out the sea.
Moon-veiled palazzi pale as odalisques

darken their metal window bars with kohl.
San Marco's reef of faded coral drowns—
the placid hallowed bowed by concrete crowns.
Everything wavers, sunk beyond recall

in shallow recollections. In between
the atolls of this archipelago—
their shoulders dusted with scurf of snow—
the shadows pass, too patent to be seen.

Only three atolls on a milky sea, veiled by this archipelago of giant moon-drunken masks. Then, optative water roars; the lion drowns inaudibly. All tourists a night bird shadows darken. Odalisques with coral shoulders crane their kohl-dusted recall, placid, wearing faded, hallowed crowns, pass between a few late diners bowed with sarcomas. Aboard the shallow window: insomniacs drown in these, trade their metal bars for plastic, churn out the scurf of everything too patent, too concrete. Winged snow of the Beyond, sunk in the seen, wades like jade recollections of pale palazzi, as the graveyard carnival wavers to be freer.

80. Without Face

Reflections chase reflections: shadow-plays,
rococo marionettes, Pierrots of lace.
The dead look out from husks in shop displays,
in endless onion-layers without face.

In artful déshabillé that courts applause,
the streets parade the runway of decline—
ignoring Reason's sumptuary laws—
fanning themselves: affected, pavonine.

Moulages of the past commodified,
enticements of recurrent carnivals,
disposable personae, filmy cauls.
At night a phosphorescent algal tide

imprisons, in fluorescent resin, busts
of Venuses and St Sebastians,
those mock-archaic youths in plastic casts—
the minor gods of fashion mannequins.

Without decline the endless affected themselves. At archaic layers, youths — in the fashion of gods — chase the artful law's filmy enticements. Minor personae of Venus's disposable mannequins face the recurrent scent of applause. Reason's pavonine reflections, fanning St Phosphor that, cast from those courts, play-mocks the Son, in past husks, in plastic parade a shadow-shop imprisons. Algal pier on a fluorescent lace tide. Runway streets in resin. Night carnivals of sumptuary dead. Ages moul, end commodified. Cauls rot ignoring Sebastian's displays of déshabillé. Marionettes' looks bust out of reflections — in a rococo I.

81. Purgatorio

The humbled palaces are at the troughs;
they lap at their diminishing returns.
The merchant's scales are balanced; what he earns
is what this lustrous snake forever sloughs:

the filmy future sunlight desiccates
into a handbag holding lipstick, keys.
The floating capital where currents seize
the slough — invasion that perpetuates

the death of Venice. Afterwards, the show,
a ghostly montage as the future fades
in retrospective video: arcades,
buyer's remorse in *purgatorio*,

where gradually each hungry ghost admits
what all along he knew — the merchandise
though fake, was offered at a tempting price.
Policemen light a pyre of counterfeits.

Caste dices at a slick pit. The hungry snake scales are balanced. Diminishing, humbled, the price offered, the Future returns, seizes the key in sunlight's invasion of death: all the fake palaces, the forever tempting montage of remorse the ghostly policeman perpetuates. That ghost capital admits the light gradually, fades in a pyre (a long lap, in what heat!) — a purgatorio where what merchandise merchants are holding (their bad lustrous counterfeits hang this filmy floating show, each earns at the buyer's trough) reverts to sacred poetic currents. What they knew was a video. A future Venice sloughs the slough, as though afterwards, where He is.

82. A Patient Breeze

Your forty-second birthday. Wake at eight,
answer a message, still among the quick—
the thought of death waits, hanging like a tick;
sit at a cafe, start to speculate

on rising accents, futures still in flux,
while ferries churn the froth as they depart
for San Michele. Not too late to start
heeding the seal imprinted in the wax

still redolent of flowers, buzzing fields,
blue-mantled days among the pliant blades,
eating a book, while angels play charades.
The breathing body still more deeply yields

facing the walls, aflame with cypress trees:
a city fallen sacked by broken hordes
despoiling its economies and lords,
their flag a cerecloth. Light, a patient breeze.

A too thrifty ego of light, thought, breathing. Speculate on the economies: the second, not fallen, departs while still within (by the blue-mantled answer to the message birthed among accents, flag, cerecloth, to imprint the future start more deeply in the flux), yields, hanging, facing the wall of city, book, despoiling death and its buzzing lords, tick-angels eating. A late days' still redolent wax waits at a cafe. Sacked, still the froth San Michele ferries churn at. Start, while still pliant as fields heeding a quick breeze. Shed theory; play charades. Sit for a day among patient trees (wake as a cypress) like their seal. Your broken body, rising, flowers aflame.

83. A Winning Streak

You want to sit, but all the chairs are wet,
the tables blistered. Lean mosquitos whine
like dentists making the enamel shine.
The crowds perform a stately minuet

across a ballroom only ankle deep.
When rain returns, the mossy caverns bloom:
umbrellas glow like fungi in the gloom.
Slow fades and jump cuts; you are not asleep,

but like a cardsharp shuffle points of view,
fanning the frames out, then attempt a raise;
though the casino has seen better days,
the cards allow no other avenue.

Seaweed casts shadows on the verd antique;
mould rises over frescoes like a tide.
Penurious nobles, whose deep pockets hide
steaming polenta, ride a winning streak.

The seen, a cardsharp, cuts the cards, fanning the mossy nobles (deists the tables ride glow in antique frames), shines like the making you perform, deep across the caverns of want, the mute penurious gloom. Better when you raise shadows, not like fungi but verd umbrellas. A steaming sea crowds the casino; a tide pockets returns, whose slow shuffle casts a lean ankle on the wet enamel avenue. All fade in a stately rain. Days deep asleep allow mould to bloom over the blistered ballroom frescoes. Only sit, view no other, though the attempt jump like mosquitos; weed out whine and winning; rise, hide like points, abate—an ash streak—return to *Charis*.

84. An Open World

An open world of echoes, free-to-play
(with extra content for a modest price
and in-game ads that tacitly entice—
advantages for which you have to pay).

The same few samples looping randomly
suggest an atmosphere, the textures load—
a skin of sequins masking lines of code.
The algal, rhythmic currents of the sea

support a multiplayer spectacle,
where death is not an ultimate defeat;
the dead log in, respawn but not repeat;
the architecture is procedural.

Progress to earn achievements you can save
and share with friends. Outside the streetlights bloom.
Near the Piazzale, in his blue-lit room,
a boy is killing zombies, wave by wave.

Outside the open spectacle of progress, lines of dead friends — content to code, for modest pay, a looping architecture echoes support, killing death with play, to save the game that is the world — repeat and share in the Ultimate which, to entice achievements tacitly, masking His free price in defeat, respawns *ad extra* the same sample of skin lit by the Text. Not a procedural Santa, a Loa with random advantages for the few zombies in sequins, but a rhythmic multiplayer bloom of lights you cannot earn, lucid blue atmosphere wherein is room, a sea surge, wave on wave — and *you* is a near analog that suggests all currents.

85. The Mall at Night

Of late you have preferred the mall at night
just where its neon leaks into the sea,
a cafe lit up like a pharmacy,
to watch masked stragglers and attempt to write.

The busy bar next door plays 80's pop;
a vaporetto passes like a float,
slow as your gaze across the lines you wrote
this morning in a mirrored ferry stop.

There is a lurid yellow post-machine,
across from you, beneath a frosted lamp—
where you might buy an envelope or stamp,
tapping the foreign symbols on the screen—

and then a Co-Op down the spacious street
where checkout women (glossy in the chill
fluorescence) patter on the till
like harpsichordists playing with their feet.

This just in: neon symbols float across a glossy screen, like a gaze where a chill, pop fluorescence plays on and on, from a 0 like a vapour — across the within — to ∞. Write, then post, the lines where you lit up. The feet you wrote patter down to the next busy cafe or bar, as a haven where the masked and mirrored check out their like, leak coin. You might still stop, attempt to watch the buy-it-machine playing you; beneath your preferred lurid mall, there is a slow spacious foreign street. Night: a yellow lamp stamps the sea's envelope. Of a morning, women tapping at the frosted pharmacy door. The orchardists' ship passes to ferry late poet stragglers.

86. Discriminating Eyes

After a year, we meet again. I stall
swiping at names; he tactfully relents,
lifts up his shirt to show his documents:
the stomach, branded like an animal,

arms stamped in Libya with cigarettes.
He speaks of nights in pens of reeking goats,
of desert journeys and of rusted boats.
As if attention could absolve these debts,

I nod and search my pockets for a word
threadbare enough to flatter his disguise —
conscience has such discriminating eyes.
Both of us recall a summer vineyard:

my youthful month spent in the clustered rows,
his only paying work for many years;
I think of blind hands wielding secateurs,
and dark juice stinging cuts that will not close.

Goats stamped in night's dark stomach. O, a journey's threadbare pockets! Summer, wielding stinging cigarettes, relents, after his shirt shows a rusted juice and his eyes close, blind. The discriminating swiping, paying for youthful branded years (clustered, reeking in boats, rows of pens, these will work off debts, off at a desert vineyard, with ably animal-like secateurs, documents that my hands cut). We tactfully search for His nod, to absolve again month, year. Attention spent to flatter conscience. Enough! He lifts up His arms. I think, I stall in my disguise. As both of us, I and not I, the Word speaks many such meet names, only He could recall and fashion.

87. Elvis

I told you, Elvis says, *did you forget?*
I'm living in Vicenza, as I said,
he says. And words unravel, as the thread
of language catches on the barbs of debt.

He sits beside me, as we face the square
where night and day manoeuvre kings and pawns.
Such scraps of words as flutter on the thorns,
in this dead garden, ripple as they tear:

Do you not recognise me? Words arrange
themselves like objects on a table: pen,
book, coffee cup, right hand; my left — unseen
inside a pocket — worries beads of change.

Now I will leave you, he gets up and goes.
The sky beyond the awning growing dim,
I sit there — trying to remember him —
becoming colder, till the cafes close.

As told, I arrange such barbs of dust as, say: coffee, hand, table, Vicenza... till I forget: Did I leave you, or you me? There goes the thread, I said, and catches on you. Elvis sits and worries. He says, I'm dead. And he gets up, as they flutter beside him, ripple unseen, unravel scraps, as waning night beads in words on the king's thorns. Language, in debt, pawns objects, pockets change. He left me this cup. On a dim day, I sit and pen my book. The garden will close inside you, where words square words, growing colder beyond the sky—a tear of the living Now—becoming like themselves, trying to recognise the Face of faces: as of a Man, the oeuvre we do not remember.

88. Dottore, Dottore

The young men, begging at the cafe, roam.
Dottore dottore... the ribald students haze
a recent graduate who's crowned with bays;
he drags a painted cross of styrofoam

and through their mockery is reconciled—
they drive him, with their belts, across the square.
The young men get some change, then disappear.
John fled from Elsewhere, with his wife and child;

Being a Christian I could not remain
he says. *I have no other clothes to wear.*
I put my pen down, offer him a chair;
the harrowed cobblestones are glazed with rain.

His eyes are cloudy as a troubled pool
in which I waver with my crown of bays.
The students sing a mocking song of praise,
that ends with a repeated *vaffancul.*

The Other says: *I remain in being repeated, crowned with eyes; men fled my offer, they waver through change, disappear with the rain some haze drags across a cloudy pool.* I / not-I are reconciled in Him, who put on a mocking crown His own cobbled. Young men roam, begging for their wife and child. Elsewhere, my mockery drives Christ to His cross. The troubled song, the harrowed praise, are from Him. A students' cafe: the young have salad with chai; the graduate students wear belts with recent clothes, pen then sing their ribald bays, with a *dottore dottore*, a *vaffancul*. The square of painted styrofoam ends with a gate of stone. John is that at and by which he gazes, as could I.

89. Ospedale al Mare

When we arrive, the former hospital
is open for a tour, the guide awaits:
a young Nigerian, fallen between states.
We follow him along a sunburnt hall

(the plaster peels like skin where summer glares)
past rooms of records lying in white dust,
into the basement where the boilers rust,
and out again to face a flight of stairs.

Someone set fire to his sometime room.
Outside is bright; inside this cindered cave
he lost what little he had left to save.
The past diffused then like a diesel fume.

Now he has moved onto a higher floor:
facing the Adriatic, broken glass
for parquetry, his mattress stuffed with grass,
a shopping trolley pushed against the door.

When a shopping trolley peels rust onto grass, diesel boilers fume, what past to save? This statement is lying... We moved higher again—where the lost regal Now awaits, a triadic Someone—facing the face of the sun, summer diffused along His skin. We, His heathen young, fallen in broken plaster into time's hospital, a bright glass between inside and outside, to arrive against the cave's base: a parquetry floor where ash, a cindered dust of matter some former fire had left, is, like all, like Him. Follow the tour guide out, past the white stairs of flight, to the little set, a room of rooms, stuffed with burnt records. For Her, He—reining—has pushed the door open...

90. Ghosts of Carnival

A vendor pushes racks of jangling masks
along the smudged pearl of the waterfront.
Forms bear the fog's entire formless brunt;
light spills out of the street lamps' broken casks.

The wayward ghosts of carnival emerge
out of the marble dust, the plaster haze
(you hear the sculptor chipping at a frieze,
struggling against the sea's erasing surge)

their masks adorned with icy bells of dew;
their eyes a fog-bound darkness, crinoline
hoop-skirts and ruffles hide their coats of skin.
They roam the gloaming, pause and pose in view

of the Basilica's facade — a monochrome
nocturne by Whistler, or a pale Monet —
and then depart, but seasonally fey,
on neon ships into the drizzled foam.

The facade-vendor skirts the smudged street and, seasonally, pushes casks of dust, eyes the racks of the fey bound with neon hoop. Their bells broken, in view of the waterfront, as their pearl ships depart into the gloaming. Skin masks the wayward masks; they hear the icy ping by a monochrome carnival of ghosts. The sea's dew-adorned nocturne — jangling against the marble you pose, pale sculptor, inner Clio — ruffles the entire plaster frieze. The formless and their coats roam a brunt erasing foam basilicas. Bare forms, struggling out of fog, chip at fog, emerge along or out of a pause. Darkness and light hide Mt One. But, then, a surge of haze spills on the drizzled lamps of Whistler.

91. The Junk Armada

Under the bridges, where the limpets cling
to slick green shadows, are the tethered boats,
far from the ladies dangling perfumed stoats:
the junk armada of a fallen king,

waiting the rain out under plastic tarps,
bent over boiling rice or bitter tea
on braziers of smouldering debris;
old men with crutches made of broken harps;

young women cradling bundles of despair,
open mouths mewling for an ashy breast;
the guarded fathers at their shallow rest,
lean navigators who, unsleeping, stare

into the distance or consult their charts
by the cracked radiance of tablet screens.
While, ministering to the sick, Beguines—
in plastic habits—ply their healing arts.

Slick young women, in stoats, cracked plastic mouths guarded, cradling habits, while bitter old men consult charts of a breast. Bent under green despair, tethered by the ministering distance, the radiance navigators ply their crutches. *To be* boiling over. Under the far off tablet, an unsleeping stare. Waiting for rain, shadows broken open, sick with the plastic debris the shallow genius of the ashy king made. Smouldering ladies dangling from estate bridges, the limp fathers of the armada cling to their fallen harps or lean on junk, mewling at the healing screens, where the arts are bizarre traps. O who cries out or bundles the rest into their perfumed boats?

92. Weaving the Veils

The glut of radiant marble makes you sick;
but still you have to walk and beg for sense,
exchange fluorescent sycamores for cents.
You still have time to sell a selfie-stick,

before the final train departs with all on board:
the beggars propping up *palazzi,* mute
men with unwanted roses who commute
back to the warehouse where the world is stored,

the contract workers slowly going blind
weaving the veils of velleity,
inside the sweatshops of the hyper-city,
repeating patterns someone else designed.

The others, free to walk and hesitate,
watch broken shadows cross the Bridge of Sighs
where, with a fan, stern justice shields her eyes
from those devoured by the *mask of state*.

From the bridge, fan her with the scent of the still sycamores. Before the unwanted world of others, beg the roses — radiant sighs, shields of velleity, beggars of veils. Hesitate to board a blind train going back to state *palazzi*. Stern hyper-exchange workers have to sell on the side. Walk slowly, repeating patterns; but, the fluorescent city departs. Watch mute, broken shadows weaving a contract designed for propping the final men, who have to sweat in the glut warehouse (where else?). Time is devoured, and the selfie-someone shops for stored sense. You make those still sick free of the marble mask and stick. All walk with eyes up by the Cross, where you commute justice with You.

93. The Smallest Crumb

I tell the pigeons there is nothing more;
perhaps they have some idiomatic phrase
for begging crumbs on hazy winter days,
when finely chiselled hunger, without flaw,

with metal spikes across its salt facade
towers above them. I cannot translate
their ruffled utterance as grey as slate,
nor read the stanzas where their tattered bard,

mangy and hopping on one scabrous foot,
sings of their bondage and deliverance,
when they will leave behind their nomad tents
in long, ragged procession, having put

the grave, paved streets behind them. I attempt
to show the empty plate; on stealthy claw
they scavenge, test the patience of the law,
from which the smallest crumb is not exempt.

Stealthy, plate metal pigeons, above, test their finely chiselled towers, their hazy spikes. Begging the street paved in scabrous slate, long days patience on mangy foot will cross tattered leaves, scavenge winter salt, having put on the ragged show. A flaw-exempt bard, sings one phrase behind stanzas of ruffled utterance I translate. The smallest crumb's crumb is deliverance from bondage to nothing — hunger of the empty grave, the not without, which cannot read nor tell them, when they claw their tents, when they attempt hoping for more: perhaps some idiomatic nomad, behind the law (its grey facade), there where They is and with Them, Their sap and procession, I have the I, a son.

94. Image Filter

Rain strips appearances to shades of grey;
patches of colour pop as if they were
isolated by an image filter;
the garish present seems an overlay

superimposed on a daguerrotype.
Itinerants in plastic robes like monks
follow a monstrance; on their narrow bunks,
the homeless huddle at the doors of sleep,

while their familiars, the pigeons, doss —
too drenched to fly — on vacant window sills.
Dispersed by wind, untethered cafe bills
scatter like thoughts, adhere to silver gloss.

After a while, when the deluge clears,
a waiter prods the awnings to set free
their burden — cascades of transparency —
so a prismatic covenant appears.

While monks, in their garish plastic robes, wait on the homeless itinerants, they huddle at the doors of images, drenched by a free transparency—while the deluge renews their present, cascades, appears as the appearances, set on silver, scatter untethered. Overlays of thought. Dispersed, isolated shades adhere to their vacant covenant, follow familiar like pigeons, strip to burden a narrow bunk, faces superimposed—soon after, sleep patches their ills. While, when a wind fills a window, the grey trance of the argued clears, like rain. By an awning a gloss of colour filters, prismatic drops pop; to boot, poetry seems to arise, fly, dons moss.

95. Emerald Tablet

I met him in Ikea once; he held a frame
in his right hand, and in his left a roll
of smuggled Soviet posters like a scroll
of Hebrew letters flickering with flame

beneath the lamp of Isaac Luria.
He flourished it discreetly, eyes aglow:
the old performance, played *con spirito*,
as full of rumours as the Curia,

spinning a karmic web from dental floss
(tea with Kropotkin and a Russian blonde
who knew her Hegel), like a portly Bond
with silver cufflinks of the Rosy Cross.

He introduced us, indirectly. Called,
and said that we would do each other good;
he had our numbers. Now, that rumpled god
swipes left his tablet made of emerald.

Posters scroll the web with a hand-held tablet, spinning emerald rumours, and a Rick roll. A blond Russian, that flourished in the old Soviet curia, swipes silver cufflinks from a crumpled frame. God called, had Isaac bound. He who said I am, within each of us, left the Spirit discreetly as He left. Our flickering eyes do flame, on Ikea St, with that full Now of loss. His performance of the Good, smuggled in letters, numbers. Hegel and Kropotkin played a hand beneath His Cross. We once knew of Her, of His rosy Other: a lamp aglow, introduced indirectly, as Her web of like made like. Poor tinselled Atman; if the Liar ate rightly, and met Him, he would submit.

96. A Roaring Shell

Running behind me, naked, (I was bound
not to look back) you dove into the swirl
of plateresque, alloy of seal and girl.
And I obeyed that slender chain of sound

till you were under: just our heads above
the silver platter; all I could not say
below—you dancing, veiled like Salome.
Later we slept, our backs against a grave

—the sea below us, gnawing at the scar—
not lovers yet, you only keeping warm,
the plaster fluid in a perfect form,
the future dead already like a star,

and we, pinned by its keen, delayed farewell
like butterflies on inky velvet, seen
inside a Venice shop, an old vitrine,
together with an empty, roaring shell.

You and I were warm alloy, our just later form — you and me — delayed in an inky look: I like I against you like you, pinned together at the scar of the seen. We could not say it, slept naked, empty inside a roaring swirl of gnawing butterflies that veiled us, dead lovers with plaster heads. Our only sound was running, bound to a perfect future by the velvet chain of farewell. The girl keeping shop behind Venice, already under a vitrine. Below: an old sea-shell platter. Plateresque Salome, slender, silver back dancing on a grave. We dove, fluid like seals, back into the not-yet-not — till all obeyed, above and below, the keen stars.

97. Fabric Scraps

You were the still point of a touring storm,
a cyclone of couture and fabric scraps,
ripping the roofs off cosy rodent traps,
invading in a patchwork uniform

the sober desert of my mud-brick cell:
camp followers of faded lingerie
tempting my books to leave their ordered fray;
swirling around the vestibule of hell —

the listless things that did not dare to choose
but simply maundered in your ruffled wake,
saved from the outer darkness by mistake
or by inertia; your long line of shoes

like souls queued up by dismal Acheron.
Your essence is in infinite regress;
of burning rags is sewn your wedding dress,
I loved a garment you tried, briefly, on.

The listless id, touring around hell, maunders by mistake. A dismal mud traps my dress shoes. Queued, I camp briefly by swirling Acheron, wake in that infinite burning desert — i.e. the cosy outer vestibule of love — saved in a faded bricked-off cell, the I. My sober patchwork of scraps, sewn by ripping up books to storm the wedding. Long regress from things, their tempting inertia, to dare fray the uniform fabric. Darkness is not simply a point, but a line of rodent followers invading your lids. Your soul's still garment ruffled. You did choose torture; linger on or leave the cyclone, like you were, in your ordered rags, and you're cured of the essence of of of...

98. Narratives of Fate

See little Caesar with a sharp-tongued moll
named Cleopatra, in a rug let soak
in sloe-gin, sex and apple-scented smoke:
you waited for my order to unroll;

it never came or, rather, came too late.
You greeted me, in your most candid face —
no stale confetti of the commonplace —
adorned with starlit narratives of fate

and we performed the rite with eyes wide shut:
hieratic poses on a rented bed,
to summon spirits till the Spirit fled.
The magic worked. That day the bond was cut

between that other pair, who briefly cried
forever and forever. They awoke,
ignorant what Dramatis Personae spoke,
to find the ink upon their contract dried.

You, sole-most, worked in no other the rite of day, the late starlit magic, till the apple briefly cut the bond. Summon the pair that fled to sex, shut too wide their commonplace eyes; contract Your forever between order and smoke. Cleopatra waited in a rug or cried, gin-tongued, on a stale scented bed, greeted Caesar adorned with poses, a dried face. They came sharp and candid, performed ignorant personae to find, rather, that spirits awoke to see it—the confetti moth of will, upon what never was spirit. Who spoke and named me with my hieratic little rented fate, its drama let soak in ink? You came for narratives we unroll forever.

99. Shuffling Masks

At night, it overflows the wells and lies
in silver pools — time's tensile mercury;
the slippery afterbirth of memory,
remains to feed on when the infant dies.

A photo of her pausing on the stairs:
the backwards gaze — the order disobeyed —
that lifts from darkness one implicit shade,
before returning to the world's affairs.

The image moulders like a sodden page
found in the corner of a toilet stall:
bodies, disjointed as a Bellmer doll,
consume each other in a carnal rage;

the void lies yawning under shuffling masks,
his jackboots by the bed — as Duse twists
beneath D'Annunzio, who grips her wrists
before returning to the higher tasks.

The higher other, before the before, who disobeyed, dies as a shuffling, carnal doll, beneath the One that overflows in the infant image. It moulders in the slippery wells of lies, when the rage of order grips the after-birth of the void and memory lies, mercury-sodden, twists abed to feed the world's darkness from her yawning wrists. Night, in a corner, pausing at her toilet, lifts a photo. Tasks, affairs stall. The shade pools on the page, as tensile remains, disjointed under time's jackboots, found by His backwards gaze to consume the masks: D'Annunzio, Duse, Bellmer, each returning on alike silver stairs, returning to implicit bodies.

100. A Blink

Out of his mind on ice, I heard him shout
before they tasered him — a mirror-flake.
Did they remove an organ by mistake?
I had imagined gradual fading out

and not a blink, first death by which the eyes,
deprived of vision, passed the interval
of darkness before judgement, like a hole
in time, black fire purging memories.

No pennies could melt peepholes in the frost
on the old windows where we used to sit,
reading the same book, though in separate
rooms, in the simple winter sunlight, lost

within the mutual solitude of words.
You left me safe within a morphine trance;
your red shoes grabbed you and ran off to dance,
and I passed on beyond the reindeer herds.

I left You, though no rein grabbed me—the first mistake, the trance of sin—to winter in a desert where peoples groan. They sit by the red lake, orphaned by Your gradual remove. Death herds lost words before him with a shout; a simple sunlight and a purging fire melt the mirror interval of time, in judgement of us, separate and same. We heard Him reading out His book, before the darkness passed; deprived of memories, in mutual vision safe, out beyond the fading frost on eyes like windows, the black ice of solitude within a blink. You ran to me; in old shoes I could dance, and did not mind I had passed the I-hole: on and on the reed pen imagined rooms...

PART THREE

These forms once so well-behaved
obedient always ready to receive
the dead matter of poetry
frightened by fire and the smell of blood
have broken out and dispersed
       — Tadeusz Różewicz

... there are no words for the surface, that is,
No words to say what it really is, that it is not
Superficial but a visible core ...
       — John Ashbery

... actually, we neither go anywhere, nor come from anywhere, but merely expand and contract on the surface, all the while remaining on the same plane.
       — Andrei Bely

101. Rooms of Mannequins

You were much older, I was seventeen;
I took you to a Fringe show. They had made
a maze inside a warehouse: shade led shade
through utter darkness, guiding an unseen

Eurydice towards the exit door.
Lost in blind alleys we found couples, deep
within the spiral of a fingertip,
brushing the black silk of a corridor.

I grope to recollect how fingers found
themselves entwined like roots or which hand first
(deaf, dumb and blind) yielded to language: *thirst*,
spelled out in water shining underground...

that's where, each time, the memory begins
to melt like celluloid, a film-noir frame:
an empty warehouse; having lost the Dame,
I chase a thief through rooms of mannequins.

Dumb mannequins, entwined in language, like Eurydice grope to recollect the lost shining show the first thief took, inside which each I found I, amazed, begins a blind chase towards You — through a door frame, a film-noir corridor, empty rooms of the underground warehouse warehouse in even, tense darkness, where a deaf idol was found. Time, like the silk fringe of Dame Memory, brushing deep black water, a spiral of the lost — shade couples with shade, they melt I to I. That's how all, having yielded themselves in You spell out a made and utter Yes. An unseen hand, guiding — finger to fingertip or cells — we had blind roots, were led to an older exit.

102. Convalescent Lovers

Here convalescent lovers find no peace,
through disinfected wards of winter mist
shuffling in gowns with perfume at the wrist.
The cafe-band reprises *Für Elise*;

and I recall how, wanting for a bed
away from prying eyes, one night, we went
among blue paperbarks and pitched our tent
by pegging down a golf-course sky instead—

a silk pavilion, where we dined unseen,
protected from the wind by wine and skin,
playing at concubine and Saladin,
but woke up freezing on a patchy green,

huddling till dawn ignited ashen bush.
The hospital beside the sea now hosts
a stray dog guarding plaster-dusted ghosts,
rose-peddling beggars from the Hindu Kush.

From among the dawn host, in rose-silk tents pitched by the shuffling green sea, I woke up (how else?) finding, instead of peace, one plaster wind egg. I recall and paint dusty beggars, freezing and guarding a patched wineskin, wanting mist for concubine and night-hospital perfume. The disinfected now, ignited by a blue winter sky. Ashen lovers huddling in the unseen paper pavilion, prying wards away from a protected bed. Through here we went, still convalescent — stray ghosts peddling kush beside a cafe down at the course, where we dined on salad, playing golf with no HUD — but a band from the bush reprises dog-fur gowns, barks and eyes our writ.

103. First View

There's no first view of Venice. Long before
you came to claim her, Goethe spent his praise
on the dimensions of these alleyways,
as if she were some naked-breasted whore

who stands, upon a crumbling bridge, to flaunt
the domes that rise above white, chiselled cloth,
fluttering eyelids like a dying moth
circling a flame that gutters on a gaunt

and shrivelled candle dripping sickly wax.
Back then, already, she was past her prime,
abandoned to the lechery of time;
her face and body the eternal wrecks

of beauty no remembrance resurrects;
forever but a rumour of the waves
that dirge her dead armada, rock her graves—
mere pillow talk in vanished dialects.

You claim the mere body of talk is a whore: gaunt, sickly, abandoned to the waves of the past, like Goethe dying on his pillow—before long dead eyelids chiselled as graves, the candle flame vanished, face but shrivelled wax already dripping rumour on cloth. No, no, Her bridge stands, a rock. In naked remembrance, time forever resurrects eternal beauty. Rise, then, upon some fluttering moth of praise, and above wrecks that were her white armada—these alleyways that, if crumbling, flaunt her dirge of spent dialects and breasted domes and circling gutters—and back to the first and prime view of who she was there: Venice!

104. Married to Water

It's like one thing that moistly interlocks
on cool, white sheets and with a moan of gulls;
the taut waves slap the seven-coated hulls
of gondolas asleep beneath stone clocks,

with just a hint of salt, in long array.
Across the marble headboard—a silk scarf;
below, the guests at the casino laugh.
Married to water, the foundations stray.

The moon is in the window; like the steam
that dulls a bathroom mirror, clouds obscure
the sky's reflection on the mirror, pure—
the absence of the dreamer in the dream,

its failure to attain what has been lost:
that court where nothing is nor is undone,
no angels hang like washing in the sun,
and there is no one yet to bear the cost.

It's like a failure of foundations. In that stone room, with the sun washing the marble, the One that is not gulls reflection. The white sheets yet laugh; there mirror is asleep in mirror, nothing with thing interlocks. What has been dulls the dream window. At the casino below, obscure beneath the moon, the stray steam, bored, waves its silk scarf, and seven gondolas, in a long array of hulls salt had coated, bear — across a taut sky — just a hint of Her, as the lost clocks moan and the cool angels slap on the cost. In that bath water is the I most married to the Only, to attain the one court of absence no no is like to, dreamer, where pure guests hang undone like clouds.

105. Metropole

The neon landing of the Metropole:
a water taxi docks to disembark
souls borne here floating through pre-natal dark.
You hear them coming from behind a wall:

the creaks and slaps, aquatic sounds of sex;
the piers rock steadily like marriage beds,
where wives as wooden as ship's figureheads
embrace the captains of encrusted wrecks

on waves of satin, above mud and muck,
the bed posts ebony with hints of gilt.
(A Lenten moon kneels high upon a stilt.)
The finest courtesan is Lady Luck:

the reading starts when all the cards are laid
face up; she shuffles once each patron leaves —
another subtle gambler who believes
the fortunes she has cast are really made.

The metropole, steadily made of mud and luck, on encrusted stilts aquatic muck slaps. The captains disembark, at a taxi dock, as piers creak, wrecks rock. These believe a lady reading fortunes, who shuffles leaves. When figures are laid up like cards, next to another them, wooden souls, borne upon beds, pre-embrace. Alas, behind the marriage bed is a wall of heads. Gamblers' wives hear each cast landing from high above. The finest ships of the moon, floating on ebony waters; hints of a gilt sheen coming through the face of the waves' subtle ashen patron. Once sound really stops, all starts, here where You are, and the courtesan kneels in the dark.

106. The Fledgling Dead

Crossing a bridge, intent on reveries,
I met the now immortal Casanova,
masked as a migrant-worker from Moldova;
his cover — picking fruit for overseas

export among the orchards of Murano.
He'd lost his figure long ago, but kept
the old bravado, proving quite adept
at passing for a latter-day d'Abano.

He made confession — having praised my choice
of costume, rather than an alchemist
I had adopted the Armenian priest
who tutored Byron — in a muffled voice

and I repaid his candour with a verse.
He seemed content with this mock pardon of
his past, declaimed *The Sail* by Lermontov;
we watch the fledgling dead arrive by hearse.

I sail Her sea. Byron and Lermontov, crossing over bridges, mourn a day that seemed past pardon. We, migrant reveries—by choice having met masked, picking a bravado costume of praised verse (a mold-alchemist, an ex-worker, a candour-adept), quite lost among the content-orchards, a muffled, but from long ago declaimed, intent of a fledgling voice adopted by His immortal figure—now arrive. The oaf, who'd mock the made with his *he he he,* had to watch the old priest proving a tutored confession. This rain aches. Later dead from this port cover my passing hearse with fruit. The Son, His art kept in abandon, He repaid: I for I. Amen.

107. The Tryst

Babet la bouquetière behind the screen
of ornate woodwork, hears the tryst begin—
call and response, a litany of sin—
confesses it the finest he has seen:

none other than M. M.—à la soubrette,
mangling the sheets between her marble thighs;
or Lady Luck, still masked and making eyes,
to bid one play the Vatican roulette—

and Casanova. Thinking atoms strike
and fall like dice, each with one face turned up.
He is poured out like wine into a cup;
then, once again, the like become unlike:

she dons her habit, nakedly conceals
her body like a fiddle in a case;
he hides the mask inside an artless face,
and takes inventory of what he feels.

Babet, inside a screen, hears like or bid; she takes the mask once again; he has her feel her thighs. Play the dice-cup of atoms and luck out, fiddle with a vatic habit, strike wood, marble, mangling the ornate inventory of the unlike like an artless roulette and begin the masked tryst: one body poured into still sheets, eyes turned up, a litany of what each Soubrette and Casanova hides behind a face. Lady, the finest making, nakedly between face seen and Fall, confesses and conceals none other than *la bouquetière*. Thinking is Alma's hem and wine-work in response. Sin it aches Thee. The call: become, like Her one Son, like *to hen*.

108. Dredgings

The ruthless light of dawn eviscerates
a ramo where a rubber colon groans:
it sucks the marrow from the city's bones
(the rich reduction of a thousand plates)

onto a barge, or bier, for burial,
along with toxic dredgings from the bed
of the canal—to give the crowded dead
more room to raise another aerial

and surf the endless channels that repeat
the docusoaps the living co-produce.
A carbon filter through which ages sluice,
where all the excess of the flooded street

by porous surfaces is purified;
cortege of the vocationally bereaved—
where even the deceivers are deceived—
escorting death's pale-blooded trophy bride.

Vocationally abed, on a rubber bier, surf the canal which sucks the marrow from dead channels, where the carbon dredgings from a burial, where even the docusoaps, sluice. Death's barge, crowded with rich deceivers that raise a thousand groans, along the endless toxic colon, purified through the ages or another aerial filter. For, where the streets of the city of ruthless surfaces are flooded by it, the excess of all-living-light, the Bride is escorting the porous bones to repeat and to co-produce the cortege of a bereaved dawn. The pale reduction deceived. Give more, palest active seers, for the blooded trophy room of *amor*.

109. A Spotless Mirror

A spotless mirror? Hardly. It is blurred
by many marks of many fingertips.
Madonna floats above her waving hips;
the virgin touch is endlessly deferred.

The *undulating serpent* of the Grand
Canal digests dejecta—what remains
of banquets that have ended down the drains.
Time drops the anchor of an ampersand.

The creaking *wicket* spins in revenue,
a rigged roulette wheel: Russian bourgeoisie
beluga flood Las Vegas on the Sea.
While rubberneckers, jostling for a view,

are clustered round the *peep show orifice*:
in being given she dissolves the *trompe
l'oeil* into a formal gaze. Duchamp
presses the game clock and returns to chess.

Duchamp is waving. Hardly we, the many marks clustered round Her, peep, clock the endlessly virgin mirror of being that returns the grand formal gaze above (on it, a sea, the undulating given of the many floats) — anon, She dissolves, drops down, presses spotless fingertips into what remains of the show: trompe l'oeil banquet, blurred digests. While a jostling flood spins by touch the serpent wheel of time, a rigged Russian roulette for mad bourgeoisie rubberneckers to game and net deferred revenue. The canal is an amper, a bulge a deject Archon-tick drains. If the creaking hips are ended, in sand or ice, save the view in a glass.

110. Ordinary Streets

The square, an amateur dramatics stage,
hosts struggling actors who are forced to teach.
Wide streets, where dream-sails are hung out to bleach.
A hidden courtyard: songbirds in a cage

tinkle like bells, inside, a carillon
struck by the muffled hammers of their hearts.
A blazing noon. With tipsy stops and starts
a sobbing woman drags her carry-on

(one wheel is broken, so the axle grates),
mascara running, in a sun-struck daze—
as if she'd just spent hours in a maze
of pitilessly ordinary streets—

stands deafened in the belfry of her skull,
convulsing briefly when the cracked bell clangs.
Suspended from a chain the bronze sun hangs,
like a church lantern, from an upturned hull.

Mascara starts running from a courtyard lout with an axe, in as-if-staged streets; struck and struck—their tipsy dramatics—her skull a lantern, a church hull cracked, she stops convulsing. Actors, sobbing pitilessly in a broken dream cage, deafened by songbirds suspended from the hidden sun, the woman drags her one bell on a chain, inside a maze of bronze bells, wide streets where muffled hearts are forced. When noon stands blazing, briefly hangs hosts of sails spent hours bleach, the just, who are turned, carry the sun struggling up like a square wheel. An ordinary amateur is hung in a belfry, hammers a carillon of clangs. The greats daze to teach. So, I knelt into the like.

111. A Shrine in Plastic

A shrine in plastic on a kitchen chair,
in a small courtyard lit by dusty sun.
A shuttered shop, after the market's done,
where masks sing in dark windows like a choir.

The Olivetti typewriter museum
exhibits three machines in blue and grey —
species of scaffolds double the display.
Fog hangs above the wharves — a pale *Te Deum,*

intoned by waves that bow in granite hoods,
trailing their beards in chaos to deface
the hour of neon and of beaded lace,
fluorescent commerce in similitudes.

The glossy dough of domes is made to rise
upon the froth of these embroidered robes.
Moonfall through shutters, as her body strobes,
pastes strips upon her face: a new disguise.

After commerce machines defaced species in scaffolds, by the froth of the chaos wharves, disguised in embroidered robes of dark plastic, in beaded blue hoods upon neon masks and dusty beards, the choir of the three-dome fog shrine bows to Her mute face, Her new intoned body hangs the lace similitudes in a fluorescent museum courtyard, where the market's glossy exhibits double in shop windows. Above, a moon, as of dough, is trailing pale sorbets upon grey waves, their rise and fall lit in strips like shutters. Display a small granite hour, in a sun-chair, in a shuttered kitchen, on a typewriter. To live it, eat of the One that made these to sing through.

112. The Foundling Voices

A spray of jasmine on a scabrous wall
like confirmandae; just a radiant few,
distracted, scratch their names into a pew.
All is response—a brief, antiphonal

choir that hovers under golden vaults,
heeding the harper of a Dead Sea psalm:
the sea's aspersions fragrantly embalm
old houses kneeling to confess their faults.

The foundling voices flutter on a line,
sunlit, like freshly laundered handkerchiefs;
they rise like incense curling into clefs.
Entranced, Rousseau invites himself to dine,

but finds the flesh unequal to the song
the maestro tinctured silence to compose,
like a perfumer who has lost his nose;
only the Emperor dares to sing along.

Rousseau laundered their handkerchiefs. To confess to the justly-embalmed emperor is on the nose. Like a perfumer, fragrantly kneeling to compose a brief sunlit line unequal to silence, but fresh like a jasmine spray in response, the maestro has incense that invites distracted flesh to rise, curling like choirs of radiant names. All the old, scabrous sea-houses flutter like the dead, under a tinctured, golden and antiphonal vault of the harper who dares sing the entranced sea's lost voices His song confirms. Along a wall: a few faults, on a pew they scratch their sea-clefs into. A foundling psalm hovers, heeding only Him to find self in aspersion.

113. Nono, Das atmende Klarsein

Drinking a soft drink—added to your order
to qualify for free delivery—
on sickly, effervescent memory
ferried across oblivion's fluid border,

at night, you glimpse the shackles of the Riva;
you click the icon in your Photos folder:
a cafe, Coca Cola napkin holder
(*the perfect ritual*). For those who grieve her

by trying to recall her maiden name—
like Dante, exiled in Ravenna—
toppled before a bas-relief Madonna
like plastic bottles (in another frame),

between a lyre's driftwood horns entwine
exhaling shades, the chorus of the sea;
a fragment of the Seventh Elegy
wavers in echo: dust, atman, the clear sign.

Click like to qualify for the *nth* photo to frame the Riva's effervescent ritual. Drinking at a caffè, your fluid *who* abates. The shorn dead, entwined, drink older relief. Atman, free of a perfect order, in a clear icon exhaling, You recall by name shades of memory dust shackles. The toppled sign wavers between the sea's soft elegy and night's raven chorus. Lyre-holder, trying to pan oblivion, grieve those ferried before you on driftwood, in Coca Cola bottles, across the border. Glimpse the Maiden in an exiled fragment, Her plastic echo — for delivery of Her sickly kin — in the Madonna, as another Eve, your like.

114. La Fabbrica Illuminata

Elsewhere and nowhere, reading *Pollen*, while
immured with icons that emit blue light
and mock the vigils of the anchorite,
you recollect the fragments of its style,

imagining: the smell of mould and mist,
fresh sheen of brine across a morning's haul,
the mausoleum silence when a pall
falls on the bones of the Evangelist

to lift again on hazy chimney stacks
like candles sputtering to stain the dome,
the cloudy morning limned in Kodachrome,
a score, as if there echoed through the cracks

Nono's *La fabbrica illuminata*,
as windy singers stir the midden heap
of desiccated voices from their sleep
and plaster butterflies begin to flutter.

A style immured in fragments. Voices, like desiccated butterflies, flutter on and haul a pall across a windy nowhere. There, on the midden heap of plaster moulds, the anchorites of the mist-limned mausoleum stir from their vigils, as sputtering candles, to do the task of the I and the singers that echo, to lift again with the hymn morning's ice-blue dome. If and when the sheen's core and tain of imagining cracks, while you tack on the chrome brine, no evangelist of elsewhere to mock fall's cloudy smell — begin the alba afresh, through the hazy pollen of sleep recollect the morning's illuminated fabric, reading icons of silence as bones emit light.

115. The Shifting Context

The narrow, oily streets like pistons drive
the sluggish, rusty engine to replace
one backdrop with another. If you brace
yourself against a line you may survive

the shifting context; but do not expect
help from the harried prompter, who repeats
in his dark corner endless names of streets
in every variant of dialect.

No choice but let the blinding light efface
the figures in the darkness of the hall
and speak the words that you do not recall,
declaim some transcendental commonplace.

The creaking that you hear is just the cords
of the fly system shifting under strain;
soon fog will fall upon the mise en scène
and stagehands will remove the plywood boards.

Replace yourself—the narrow variant streets declaim on every corner, that sluggish fog dialect—with words that survive you, and recall who you will be in the One of the Endless Names. Expect Him soon. Fly from the creaking engine of system, the harried commonplace stagehands' plywood context (up some blinding backdrop streets), the dark, oily pistons the transcendental mise en scène effaces. If choice removes another of the board's shifting figures, in the rusty halls of fall shifting, do not strain the will, like a prompt rod to drive the line on, but let the Light speak you, not just against but under darkness. Hear the Helper repeat the accord in you and say I.

116. The Hazy Light

All is augmented, what it always was;
even the hazy light is crystal clear.
Now masks are worn for more than half the year;
the maze of streets is endless, without cause.

A ritual of radical consent,
the topsy-turvy that preserves intact
the mesmerising candour of the fact
in its inversion. A clingy cerement,

appearance swathes this body as it crawls
from a cold tunnel like a butcher's fridge.
There is a toll to pay at every bridge;
you'll never catch them setting-up the stalls

however early you decide to rise.
Walk long enough and you will hear the tones
of birds with clipped wings and transparent bones,
the scratch of peacocks fanned by trembling eyes.

Will the early you consent to decide, in the hazy now? It is, it peacocks and stalls. However, every year what was enough is clipped. Rise up trembling, as the always all-transparent body, from this maze. Pay the fat butcher's toll. There, you'll walk the inversion of topsy-turvy streets, hear augmented tones. A radical appearance preserves its setting intact. Cerement swathes the ritual that crawls clear of a tunnel of cold bones, by a long worn bridge. Even the mesmerising birds, with fanned eyes and crystal wings to catch light, never catch more than the forms, half-masks. For You are without cause. The candour of the fact is endless like a dirge.

117. A Great Star

Again she sits before the empty frame,
a feather boa draped around the sheer
negligence with which she scatters here
the moulted sequins of her youthful fame.

She hears the creaking boards, the eager hush
that rises to a foaming of applause,
unwinds the cerements of her bloody gauze,
and to her latest face applies a blush.

And all at once the flashing scalpel fades,
the vertigo of nothingness becomes
merely the limpid surface that benumbs
immediate flesh to tarry with the shades.

Tonight's performance will arrest her fall—
she hears the voices wash against the stage,
the sea laid open to its final page—
a great star playing to an empty hall.

She hears the nothingness, She fades. The Fall unwinds its boa, which scatters apples, the sequins a great star moulted. A hush benumbs the empty hall, the gauze wash. The blush of her performance becomes merely the creaking fame of shades, the empty against the all, that tain-stage. She too hears the immediate applause of feather and foot, before the bloody once-laid Face and Frame, with cerements flashing, that rises with the final voices, eager will, limpid, open to the foaming sea, a sheer youthful flesh playing at her vertigo-draped surface, to arrest tonight's latest negligence. O bards, tarry again around Her. Here She sits, Her page a scalpel.

118. A Double Feature

A double-feature: Roeg's *Don't Look Now*,
Visconti's *Death in Venice*—played at once.
The viewer, kneeling, in a doubled trance.
Fear, death by water, and a ferry prow.

The resolution low, each film assumes
the flat, cell-shaded style of *Waking Life*.
A muddy daughter, cradled. Strife
of form and chaos parting darkness; fumes

pour from a chimney, as a ferry groans
across the screen, the intervals of cuts.
Later, the god will look back with regrets,
dispersed in anime, on mobile phones,

express the hope, during an interview,
to meet his son again. A woman smiles,
with milky eyes, out of the mirror. Piles,
in mud, nail down the advent of the new.

God groans, kneeling in the form of mud, to pour the New out in each cell, parting with the Now, assumes a will doubled in low water; during the mobile mirror-trance, meets the double—shaded hope, daughter of the Woman—and fear of death, later nailed across intervals. Death cradled His Son, as life dispersed, down in the darkness by the chaos fumes. Phones play with anime eyes; vices connive on a flat screen. It smiles back at once from strife's muddy gore piles and a chimney. Resolution: don't ferry regrets, rue fate, express mere style. A viewer, waking again in the look of a look, an advent of the Everwit. A ferry prow cuts a milky film.

119. De Saliba, Annunciata

The angel stands beyond the picture frame,
his feathers clattering like cuttlebone;
her lapis dress is more like chiselled stone
than tender mantle. No address could claim

that open pause, her veil pinned by one hand,
the limpid gaze of a geometer
renouncing any rest till she can square
the circle, bowed and drawing in the sand.

Inscribed on the ecliptic, silent lips —
like still unbroken vessels — overflow.
As motionless as a de Chirico,
lectern and book wait on her fingertips.

The angel shuffles. Her raised hand forbids
all but this choice, implacable election;
she nurses her impossible conception,
as the sea echoes in her polished lids.

Her veil like conception. Tender address. Impossible open pause, renouncing the silent choice in no drawing inscribed. Her all-one unbroken sea, beyond the implacable stone that forbids, as the limpid sand overflows Her lids, Her lapis gaze — motionless election. The geometer shuffles, bowed by chiselled echoes; lips clattering as his fingertips mantle the ecliptic, a square angel stands, hand on a cuttlebone lectern, but polished picture-book raised: Her dress, as She is, like-on-like and more than the circle of feathers. In this frame, wait angel, dice, choir, and the still pinned hand, till She can nurse the vessels. Any could claim Her rest.

120. Drab Ecstasies

Morandi, had he lived here, could have caught
drab ecstasies of washing on a line,
within a sober and uncertain sign:
these memories of an immediate thought,

fading in some forever that arrives—
their fabric worn by use, penumbral forms,
powdery aspects that alight in storms,
cracked steps of a deduction that derives

from *ought* the merest evanescent *is*.
Barbed-wire notes hang on the rusted staves
atop a wall; the flagstones nameless graves
beside a church's vacant chrysalis

are worn away by crowds of shuffling feet.
At the right moment, if the wind should will,
its solemn, censed, procession will reveal
the sun's face shrouded in a pregnant sheet.

The merest flagstones, shrouded in immediate nameless ecstasies, are memories of the procession of the will, pregnant with forms, from the sun's barbed chrysalis. Thought steps, by right, forever atop the grave, alight. Washing its powdery face of crowds caught in a sober shuffling deduction that, in a solemn fading line, saves an evanescent moment. Here, a revised Morandi will hang on a drab wall, beside some notes on a sheet, these uncertain feet, at thought if sad, that could and should have lived. The cracked sign reveals: He that is, storms their vacant penumbral fabric of use. A church arrives, in worn aspects, censed rusted wire worn away by wind.

121. Giorgione, The Tempest

A deeper gaze reveals the *pentimenti*:
another woman bathing in the creek,
a caped man with a bundle on a stick.
The child at rest upon the breast of plenty,

deaf to the lightning bolt that tears the veil
of livid clouds, above the thrashing trees;
the mother in her scanty draperies;
soldier or shepherd, leaning in profile

upon a staff; two columns in the sun;
a building with a white bird perched above —
is it a stork, a heron or a dove? —
and silent water, flowing on and on...

what is most hidden, this the mother sees:
the crowds — that look on, as the caravans
of exiles pass — dispelling with their fans
smoke from the bonfire of the vanities.

With the two trees thrashing, the columns in water, white lightning (as a stick or a staff from above) upon livid draperies, look to the Woman above the clouds. The gaze is Her bird; it sees the Man hidden in the sun, the Aton, reveals the vanities of a scanty profile, leaning on smoke. The Dove, perched in Her breast, with silent tears dispelling another deeper veil. A bolt of rest flowing upon the crowds of exiles, a mother bathing a child in a creek; the most deaf and impenitent soldier fans the bonfire with a cape. Shepherd their caravans, Mother of Plenty, that pass on and on adoring this stork-bundle. On that, Thea, build what is.

122. Veronese, The Feast in the House of Levi

A black boy feeds the parrot of a dwarf;
off in the corner: German halberdiers;
an old man grasps a girl who disappears;
a fat man's nostril flares—from off the wharf

the wind brings rotting fish and ambergris—
his servant's nose is bleeding just by chance
of having impudently held his glance.
Seated by Jesus, Peter carves a piece

of lamb, ensuring all receive a cut.
Mine is no art of thought, the artist said,
finding himself minutely audited.
A dog ignores all but a feeding cat

whose tongue is polishing a bone he stole.
A songbird, John, fed from the Saviour's lips,
learns how to mimic the Apocalypse.
This feast is for the broken, not the whole.

A man is His apocalypse. Jesus stole the broken whole, finding all pieces in all, for Himself, from the fat glance and nostril who, of old, impudently grasps a rotting feast, at his corner of the Not, is but a foe. The Saviour's thought carves off minutely, ensuring the artist polishing off a bone disappears. The bleeding servant brings a fish, feeds John, seated Peter. His art dwarfs a just man who ignores it. A song bird, black from the bare grim mine, learns to cut his tongues on the wind a dog's nose mimics. Boy held girl—by a wharf, feeding a chance flare of heraldries—whose lips having audited, parrot: receive said manger, fed an abc by the Lamb.

123. Fecit, Fecit

Graffiti artists practice signatures,
turning a square into a gallery,
making the common space proprietary —
keeping, by means of painted ligatures,

parade-blimp palaces from floating off.
Walls are certificates of provenance,
tracing the form a city carves through chance;
like art appraisers we require proof.

Like sentences, streets end in dots of waste
a genteel lady stoops and neatly bags,
before her topiary poodle drags
her off, pursuing an eclectic taste.

The first intention here will not suffice.
Even a local doesn't own his style —
it haunts the mirror like a younger smile.
As Rilke notes, Titian wrote *fecit* twice.

We younger poodle appraisers like the gab, require proof, certificates, by proprietary art of tracing eclectic provenance, wrote sentences like blimps. A will chance haunts, carves genteel palaces, keeping graffiti off. Pursuing Her painted smile, through wastes of mirror, drags Rilke before the Lady. Her topiary forms parade neatly, a floating gallery. Style and taste are a practice, an intention, a means of turning square, street, wall, common ligatures of local space into His own city. The first Artist, not making from notes, stoops twice, in fondest signatures. Even here, the Titan's end at lake deficit, it suffices.

124. Towards an Image

Last night, drunk tourists in untimely cloaks
careered like crash-test dummies drawn
to smash against the safety glass of dawn,
beyond which barges unload artichokes

in wooden crates, or boxes full of panes,
young men in hoodies under puffer vests,
young men in doublets hauling walnut chests.
Rain-pearls from *countries where it never rains*

adorn a window full of lingerie.
Night sets aside his quill and pot of ink.
Above a puddle — where the pigeons drink
and sun transmutes to gold the leaden grey —

a tower leans and falls into itself
towards an image where the two agree,
where every object is exemplary
as in a sunlit, silent room in Delft.

Ink pearls adorn his night of never. A silent beyond itself falls, dies in a crash of images, like a young dawn which transmutes grey puddles to gold oil. Full barges, hauling tourists, lean against doubles in night's last panes, where the sun invests every window. And young exemplary men, in a sunlit top room of the glass tower two pigeons careered into, agree, above the safety of crates, boxes, walnut chests, the full set. And leaden quills drink rain as it rains in under-countries, where lies reign, where drunk men in deft cloaks were drawn toward an object to test, pound or smash it. Wooden dummies choke and hide from a fearful art's untimely hoot.

125. Brittle Larva

Hard light, hard shadow. Where their borders meet
the whole prismatic chaos is resolved
into a chart of colours, named and selved.
A crowd of people on a sunlit street:

each one a gaze's shambling avatar,
a faceless rapture riding an entranced
participant in ritual. Who danced
inside the brittle larva? From afar

a name returns that crumbled into drums
the night before, the face beneath the face,
the bodies cloaked in tailored veils of space,
as one as hosts inside ciboriums:

pale white and flaky, waiting to be stained
by wine or blood, or something in between.
Hammers of sunlight lightly damascene
the water where, this morning, nails had rained.

A crowd of people tailored this shadow before (a hard brittle larva). Riding the flaky hosts, selved by shambling street colours, their each face veils the face of the one morning that borders on chaos, named and stained where the pale Name Who rained from afar, a meet avatar cloaked in blood beneath hammer and nails, returns whole, as bodies, wine. A ritual where faceless light is resolved into prismatic waiting, inside the sunlight, participant in the rapture *between*. Entranced *as* something, one inside, chart the damascene of night, or be crumbled into white water or a gaze's sunlit space lightly danced to hard drums in an oaf's biro music.

126. Pavilions

At dusk the starlings in the palm tree sound
as if a drawer of cutlery were shut
too forcefully, or else a ribbon—cut
by squeaky scissors—fluttered to the ground.

People parade beneath the yellow trees;
their dogs are jerked aside by chains of scent.
Appearances attempt to represent
the paintings sold in neon galleries.

The shades of craftsmen from the Arsenal
wander pavilions—a conveyer belt
of images. Like Joseph Beuys in felt
the blind soul tests a nervous animal,

tapping a cane to tame the desert sphinx
whose back is mangy as a battered rug
inside some nomad tent. The fallen, snug
and fat-smeared soul becomes aware it stinks.

A battered, yellow sphinx. Shades of blind craftsmen tapping a cane — cut from the tree like, mangy trees represent — wander the neon desert of fallen images. And Joseph is sold. In the tent, the palm after-scent becomes aware, as some nervous animal soul, as the nomad appearances whose parade flutters by in galleries beneath ground. Inside the dusk-smeared soul pavilions, by the chained dog, the rug stinks. A table of cruelty's arsenal tests, as it were, squeaky people too snug in their paintings to attempt to convey the fully felt. A star-sling or sound ribbon jerked to tame force. Scissors are by use — else, if shut, die at the back of the drawer.

127. The Barnacled Colossus

Your final, fondled euro has been spent;
red lights of bars display the stockinged thighs
of streets where peacocks drag their sleepless eyes,
towards a dawn like tarnished revetment.

The paper streamers that recall the tide
wilt, near confetti like discarded scales—
jetsam of galleons with sequinned sails.
The bubbles rise together or collide

to fizz in unison and softly burst.
The square is like a diamond-studded skull;
dangling its package like a wrecking ball,
the barnacled colossus Damien Hirst

hauled with a cruise ship down the Grand Canal,
as if dragged through waste-clogged superficies,
is covered with some horny skin disease.
The craft is slick and ruthlessly banal.

The eons, like bubbles, with some bad craft first dragged thirst down towards streets like thighs softly through a stocking fondled and ruthlessly discarded, where skin is a waste of superficies covered with scales, clogged with gall, disease, age, horny then spent, banal as cruise ship bars or the tide of Red Square confetti. Peacocks collide, wreck their sequinned sails on Ulro's grand revetment. Near, the angling pack drag in the stream's studded jetsam. I, a Cain, recall the final dawn that will rise, like a colossus of lights, in the papery skull, like a sleepless diamond — to display all the sick and damned hauled clear together, as Its untarnished buzzing eyes, if our I's be Her bees.

128. The Crystal Trembles

You fade in sunlight (where the canvas ripped
to show the gold-leaf ground that burns below—
as if you'd dozed off, sleeping through the show—
gaps in the painting where a forger trapped

nature's original, rumoured destroyed
by fleeing Nazis in some cellar trove:
allegedly a naïf apple grove,
among whose clearings red gazelles strayed),

assume a shape in shadows: drapes of black
cool-handed gabardine, quite loosely cut,
just around corners where two worlds abut,
through narrow tunnels where ammoniac

memories lean, one hand against the wall,
drunkenly tinkling, as they hum a song.
The crystal trembles when that massive gong
the sun is struck, becomes provisional.

Cut against it, if trapped in a naïf canvas —
you'd strayed through massive drapes drunkenly,
to where lean memories fade, as provisional
worlds leaf loosely in that original sunlight.
The two, sleeping — when the cool, red-handed
forger struck (the painting trembles!) — narrow.
Ink shadows of gazelles among rumoured crystal
clearings, fleeing the ammoniac cellar, the ripped
gabardine, through song tunnels below a gold
wall — they, whose natures You assume, as apple
becomes grove. Where sun burns, handsome
Nazis are destroyed; but that show we dozed
in...GONG!...allegedly...HUM!...one shape
just around corners...Ground of the gaps? Quite
a trove. Whereby the show is. Glint. Ah! Fin...

129. An Endless Catalogue

Antinous leads the suitors in a toast;
Penelope unravels her design,
unweaves the threads of rain that slash the coast.
Outside of Harry's Bar the pigeons croon;

dictators waddle past with swinging canes.
Slapstick invasions — sails of black or red
float through the square on flooded windowpanes.
The rats make do with rumour's soggy bread;

they swarm the tree of alleys to the root.
A smear of moonlight on a scaling knife.
The cobbles of the *pescaria* wet
and slippery with the viscera of grief.

The shadows pick your pockets but they steal
only used tickets, incidental fluff.
Inside some cluttered basement, Joe Cornell
compiles an endless catalogue of stuff.

But Penelope unravels the viscera of Antinous, and of the slippery suitors that, flooded with moonlight, make a wet red smear. Dictators croon of invasions, waddle through. Shadows, swinging incidental cobbles, they steal windowpanes, the bread of pigeons. Black sails float. An endless rain canes the slapstick swarm scaling the airspace of grief. The fluff-cluttered coast compiles a catalogue. Harry's on tickets, Joe Cornell on the bar. They toast to the alleys, the roots of her tree. In the square, soggy basement, inside some pocket of used stuff, with rats of ado, slash with your only knife the design the past weaves, unpick rumours, threads or leads.

130. The Surface

Gaspara Stampa pauses on an arch
(near San Trovaso), which did not exist,
when she walked calli bathed in flaming mist.
Now that she wanders among leafless larch,

as birds swim past her, in the bottle green
fluorescence through which radiance descends
unsteadily, she thinks this bridge well lends
itself to watching without being seen:

pale figures walking on the other side
of the canal, traversing chiselled smoke,
or skilled calligraphers whose every stroke
perfects its gesture in a selfless glide,

knowing both sides reflect one emptiness.
She ponders, at the edge—her angling hands
caress the surface no one understands—
how one might conquer without loving less.

As one gesture, selfless birds (traversing radiance, one Now, not *other* or without Her flaming emptiness in which Being thinks itself, perfects every caress) bridge both sides of the canal, on which swim pale leafless figures watching green calli-graphers skilled at loving Her surface without knowing (how near the edge we exist!), or sons through whose hands She conquers Her past, descends, bathed in gelid fluorescence. She wanders, broken, angling a bottle; pauses, unsteadily, to smoke. Reflect this one art that ponders no stroke, a rain walking on mist. Hell understands less — it's when a vast zilch dices.

131. O Sulamita

The roaring lion's leather jaws are closed;
his tongue is lapping at an ashen *rio*.
Qui porto — she once wrote — *l'Idol mio*;
Ansaldo's queen (irreparably deposed

now) still withholds one *p* from *Copia*.
The resolution of the image fades.
Days pass. The princess solemnly parades,
across the platen of a copier.

Words of the dead. Upon his fathers' breast.
Discursive gravestone, scattered Autumn leaves
in someone's photograph. On other graves,
falling and rising images invest

the leaning tablets. Steady waves of meter.
Near, Goethe found the grave of Consul Smith.
A ticking chisel, calls to Sara with:
Torna, torna o Sulamita.

Paler now, the Queen Sofia, solemnly withholds, deposed in the arid image, idol of dead tablets. She fades upon falling, scattered as torn leaves on a gravestone, day's steady discursive ticking. Mooring at the port, the consul found waves lapping across someone's lean once-chiselled resolution to quit the passing and simulant. The torn tongue calls to an Other. Goethe also wrote of the Princess. Autumn parades near the barest Real. A mere I is a a a copy of Smith's photograph on a copier. One Father irreparably invests. His Word, a lion, still roars, rising from closed jaws, the ashen grave of graves, with His images.

132. A Lady's Fan

Goethe observes a whorling tide that leaves
a threshing floor behind it as it yields.
He stoops to gather husks the swaying fields
deliver in the breakers' foaming sheathes.

Guided among the shades by Winckelmann,
his gaze pursues the lace, beneath the hem,
Mnemosyne at last reveals to him,
before retreating with the midday sun.

He dries in shells the ink of cuttlefish,
whose signatures elude him in the shoals;
finds Smith, subject to endless burials
by windswept sand. Yet is no *nouveau riche*:

he has already seen it all laid out in plan,
atop the tower, whose one uncracked bell
still tolls in echoes of the Arsenal—
the whole unfolded like a lady's fan.

The One who reveals Him that towers atop the uncracked whole, stoops to deliver all. He has no tolls for the shades to elude, guided out by the Lady's bell, swaying among endless windswept shoals, beneath the sun's threshing gaze. He already pursues the husks of His plan, before it is unfolded in echoes. Mnemosyne yields a lace fan, whose hem dries like cuttlefish, seen by midday. Smith's shell, laid in burial, subject at last in Him, leaves behind the sheathes. Goethe observes the tide, a whorling arsenal, yet finds the breakers' signatures still in the sand retreating, to gather with ink the foaming field. Lo, the new oeuvre: a Man. I clink in a suite of chains.

133. The Tranquil Basin

There is only one form of water which is repugnant
to Régnier, and that is rain. —Havelock Ellis

The hidden gardens whisper in the dark;
the fountains trickle, near identical.
Eyes closed, Henri adjusts his monocle.
When I read Goethe, I forget Bismarck,

he writes across a mirror mist obscures,
and finds his subtle fingertip retains
a trace of dust. The fountain water drains
as blood will from a face, then disappears

down by-blow corridors, in lightless cells;
but here, the sunlight rings out as it chips
away the stone from Undine's grape-stained lips
and ivy tames the rigid pedestals.

Some days are rainier, but that will pass;
and then, among the silence we shall see
the fountains rise of yew and cypress tree,
the tranquil basin turned again to glass.

A cypress finger obscures silence's stone lips. Undine's whisper writes rings across tranquil water. He, hidden fountain of fountains, fountains down the subtle basin, disappears in His trace, I AM in the crib, turned to lightless blood corridors, but He finds it, tames the dark will, the eyes closed as cells. But, among days that pass out of mist, I forget the glass gardens, by a rigid yew tree, and read Goethe near some ivy. Rain trickles from the grape. The tip retains ark and monocle; here ire adjusts the will, and then and then drain care. See the ship blow away. When shall we rise again from the mirror, in identical sunlight, as His dust-stained faces' pedestal?

134. Dottor Serafico

He drops his glance down from the bridge as bait;
his image dangles like a marionette
from downcast fingers pale and delicate,
as Dottor Serafico deigns to wait.

Below, Gaspara reads her rotting book,
allows her perfume to entice his mind,
but does not speak, since she has met his kind
who cut the line, but don't remove the hook

before they throw the gasping minnow back.
To her, his skin tones are an open grave:
clay, blood and lime that only flame will lave,
a Deposition done by Safet Zec.

She knows the season when all passions are
withered like leaves, and burnt in compost heaps
and when the finest marble statue weeps.
His nostrils quiver at the smell of tar.

Back before Dottor Serafico met Her in Gaspara, the delicate flame — withered by habit, a grave pale mind, downcast in blood and clay — quivers as image-leaves speak: an open glance gasping at Her like. Perfume entices marble nostrils to marionette passions finest fingers dangle. Compose art or don't, as tones weep, but throw a line from His burnt bridge — the hook drops down below the skin of season and kind, that know not His design. The statue who reads his rotting book heaps — lime removes the smell. But His deposition laves all now and, since they are His, He has to wait, allow the zetetic will. Only when she's like Her, when His art's done and safe from moths, does He cut.

135. Self-Portrait

The bathroom mirror sleepily observes
what it has seen before: the succulent
eyeballs—like oysters that retain the scent
of Venus sweating—as *of one who serves*

or *of a woman*, the aspiring brows,
the mouth a mouth not hesitant to speak...
the forehead towers, but the chin is weak.
Like an armada, on whose thrusting prows

smooth wooden sirens breast a surplus fog,
the city anchors in his placid gaze.
Like Lazarus emerging from the gauze
called by the Word, obedient as a dog,

he stumbles at the threshold of his face
and falls to kneeling, vows in gondolas—
then rood-screen letters (lacy, ponderous)
in which the sign of love becomes a trace.

An eye. The Moor's vows to retain the china forehead of love. On that screen of gauze—the gondola's prow, smooth as a siren's brow. The lacy scent and succulent mouth of Venus. Sleepily aspiring in towers, the wooden city, emerging, thrusting from the mirror, becomes a ponderous armada of fog. Kneeling in what is not like the One, but in bits, by the threshold of the seen—a surplus gaze. The Word, weak at the Woman's breast, whose hesitant mouth speaks letters, has His bath, observes a dog, who called Lazarus, traces a sign (the like which likens), falls, stumbles, sweating, obedient to the rood. Archon or oyster, He serves all placid before His face.

136. The Voices of the Dead

Your last day, near the church were Rilke heard
the voices of the dead and traced the braille
of an inscription. Coffee and a stale
croissant for breakfast. Your return assured:

the tickets booked, and all your packing done,
a month of rubbish sorted into kinds,
apartment cleaned of traces and the blinds,
hazing your rented views of Venice, drawn.

But there is no return from mazing views
projecting haloes on each vacant stage,
the blinding freedom of the empty page,
the sedimenting tides of trending news —

bits fallen from a lavish feast like crumbs.
Yet still desire's fragments dance and pair;
the broken symbols of the stranger bear
the hidden name of Him who overcomes.

Each terrible week and day of the month, a mazing news page blinds. A packing pair danced on the cleaned, stale stage of an apartment. A stranger sorted coffee and breakfast, the church booked (tick!)... And yet, but for Your lavish feast of crumbs, the returns of Your voices' tides sedimenting Your name, the heart traces braille, near the assured, vacant haloes of empty freedom. Still the hidden return—from the broken and fallen, the rented symbols, the dead fragments projecting views of views of Venice on the rending thereof—is traced the last blinding inscription, all of desire's kinds drawn into Him who bears your hazing. Art's like icons come from rubbish, and it's over and done.

137. The Street of Smoke

Rich for a month, slave to the least of whims,
I read Yeats, maudlin though the pain is gone
or just seems lighter for the telamon
I've cobbled from these cold, dismembered limbs.

Who knows *their purpose in the labyrinth*
of wind that brings the trade of many seas?
Compounded of accidental phantasies,
I set each mongrel-marble on its plinth.

Once, on the Street of Smoke, I saw a man—
behind a grated window like a shrine
in which only fluorescent candles shone
on cigarette butts and a soda can—

grinding at gravestones, to the radio,
in goggles and a mask. The light was dim;
a blizzard of blank seconds covered him
in whiteness colder than all earthly snow.

Mask on, it can smoke a cigarette a month and read on... which seems only just. I've cobbled the mongrel shrine to phantasies gone in, in, in seconds. A blizzard of soda on the maudlin radio. Once I saw, was lighter, the gated marble labyrinth shone rich in whiteness. From a dim street window I goggle at their fluorescent limbs. Pain, though accidental, brings a lament for the set of all gravestones, colder than cold, compounded of blank snows, for the dismembered Man, behind the least slave who eats Him and knows each earthly plinth covered, to trade for these whims of purpose the light of so many like candles, a wind or sea grinding at the stub that I say is.

138. Unfocused Glance

The sea this morning worries at her cuffs,
as Pound did when Charles Olson met him first;
salt on her tongue, she is consumed by thirst.
Up in a corner of the sky, a zephyr puffs

like someone blowing up a child's balloon,
which he then ties up with a knot and twists
into the shapes of great aquatic beasts.
She finds the day too much, is soused by noon.

Just close your eyes: you hear the ice cubes clink.
As opalescent as a glass of gin
and tonic, hissing, is the sky within
the hazy wakefulness of her *I think* . . .

that trails off in a long, unspoken list
of thoughts, like flotsam, that arrive by chance.
She has a steely but unfocused glance,
as if she kept forgetting to exist.

She is with the One, of old, when He shapes the beasts like a child's balloon, as a hissing tongue twists and ties thought up in a knot. And I arrive, glance up at a noon sky by Him unspoken, forgetting the sky within — the great wakefulness I share, blowing on the first morning, as you met Her by a sea of glass. But, in your corner of the clink of close cubes, Pound has an off day. Zephyr puffs ice. Some steely son, the tonic of worries consumed, eyes her, soused; just like that, he finds a chance (too much salt) to cuff her. To exist is unfocused thirst, as long as this hazy flotsam kept up by larches, that opalescent aquatic list which She trails, of which if/then is shed thinking. She is.

139. The Sudden Absence

A sun bleached campo: pigeons mill for crumbs
dropped from a window on the second floor.
The sewer rats swim past the sinking door.
At first, the sudden absence only numbs:

everything, flat and overly exposed,
seems to recede as if, hosed down and dried,
the *pescaria* halls had ossified.
All of the extras, casually posed,

idle in scripted animation loops.
Commuters wait in swaying photo-booths;
St Mark's, in flashes, is a swarm of moths.
Silent men tend the hidden pigeon coops,

however, mending when the sawdust leaks
beneath a wing, recycling shuttlecocks
for feathers to repair the cobbled flocks,
dismantling broken fountain pens for beaks.

When hosed down, a swarm of silent swaying men flashes in the sun; all had to wait at *Camp O* for dismantling and repair, be exposed in bleached mending-booths. The past, a broken sewer. Scoops tend to numb idle pens. Crumbs dropped for pigeons, the recycling animation loops. St Mark's—a sawdust floor, moths mill beneath the first window—casually leaks commuters. Rats swim; on cobbled wing, locusts flock in pigeon airspace. However, everything's extra; for, the flat second photo, posed sketch, is only the ossified door. And the hidden halls of the *as if*, seem to recede from absence. A sudden fountain: dried feathers, overly scripted sinking.

140. The Aldine Press

The Aldine press impresses Attic grace
on tides of paper, battered book debris;
dolphin and anchor on a frontispiece
sport in the lather of mendacity.

Dead fish and flotsam ride the plushy foam
that gnaws at form, too briefly luminous.
Soft fingers read the Paper Nautilus
and touch the hidden rigging of a name

that hoists this sail of calcium carbonate
to ply its trade on insubstantial seas,
from Alpha borne by ghostly argosies
unto Omega—endless change of state.

The cityscape, a row of Aldine type,
leans over nothing with elaborate poise.
Exposed, this crèche of gaudy coral toys
blanches, dissolving like a bar of soap.

Too briefly elaborate the hidden luminous alphatype, that blanches paper argosies in this attic crèche. From nothing, a rigging of form, battered by the sea's grace, hoists the paper sail of a book exposed dead read over with ghostly, coral fingers that touch this insubstantial dissolving frontispiece. Denial impresses denial. Lather of state press, and of sport on soft at a bar. Borne on tides of poise, toys ride, row, trade gaudy fish and anchor on plushy soap foam. Its flotsam gnaws a cityscape of debris, of calcium carbonate lean-tos, to mend the city. Change—like dolphin and nautilus, a ply of the Omega—unto the endless Name.

141. The Friday Book

It is not known what became of Hakob, whether
the characters that he had engraved were... later
reutilized. —Marzo Magno

The *Friday Book* of Hakob Meghapart
(a text Armenian merchants might peruse,
while asking at the market after news
of when the next flotilla will depart)—

the first book printed in that script fragments;
the moving type submits to variations:
long excerpts from the Book of Lamentations,
prayers for the sick, and cures for ailments.

With Pascal Aucher at the monastery,
in Byron's mind the sediment is stirred
and strands of seaweed curl into a word;
the page soon buzzes like an apiary,

as from their matrix of still fragrant wax
the images begin to raid the fields,
returning gilded with their dusty yields.
Your map: a mildewed wall, described by cracks.

By moving the first type is stirred, fragments in variations when returning from, with, and into the Word. Hand, printed in the wax matrix; an excerpt departs while still the book a next page describes. Book merchants at market peruse their book of mildewed images. The sediment mind forgot yields the long drone of lamentations; fields of seaweed strand the fragrant flotilla of prayers. A Friday apart. Soon after, the dusty wall will begin to crack with the New, from Your might that raids sick text, cures by their asking for a cure. A script that curls like the hem of a marine map Hakob clasps. Gilded as an apiary the monastery buzzes.

142. A Gondellied

Beside the bridge, the night parades in brown;
from far away the golden drops of song
set ripples welling on a brazen gong,
and chaos passes in his ivy crown.

His soul, a liar, singing to itself
a *Gondellied*—where light and music meet
opposing tides of bare, ecstatic feet,
and silence sniffs the future like a wolf,

who cannot find the clearing where he left
his pile of clothes. Resenting the divine,
Prometheus invites the bird to dine,
yet still remains beholden to his theft.

If life is but a battleground of tastes,
still it may yield to subtle commissars
who scan the trembling barcodes made of scars
that mark the slaves who flee the Libyan wastes.

Divine crown, beholden to no night. Scars of silence. Cross and nail maim—yield His ecstatic remains. In a subtle theft, He invites the soul to a slave's trembling, in the bare clearing of the gelid light-resenting wastes. Scan the battleground, where the brazen liar, who cannot find his feet, parades a gong. And the future still ripples from the meet drops of His brow's welling life; who tastes of it—led to flee the pile left beside the wolf who sniffs but itself—passes by a golden bridge ivy chaos clothes. Still opposing, Prometheus may yet dine on His mark, where far away singing is made a birdsong, and the brocades of tides liken, if set to that music.

143. The Blush of Art

His lips are stained and moist; he can't depart
(in neutral halls, chaste statues start to sweat
as gently as Plotinus when in thought),
pale cheeks now rosy with the blush of art.

The deckchair-stretcher waits to carry him
to wards where ether-scented angels moult,
where tidal spirits leave a trace of salt
as if around a cocktail glass's rim.

You lay the book down, order food online.
Dark algae fill the lungs of memory:
of Adriana, hanging from a tree,
Ernest retiring to his room with wine,

or Baron Corvo in an anchored shoe,
his pages lost to wind or water rat.
You and your image, in the other flat—
one pane, two fingers bound by superglue.

From the angel orders — around the lost chaste Now, where coos hover — moult thought's pale images. Rosy scented fingers of wind gently trace pages ablush with wine. Spirits, neutral or dark, if anchored to a statue, stretcher or line, moor. When you depart — to drain a cocktail in a deck-chair, by the rim of a water-pane (flat tidal glass bound in the salt of memory), retiring to a book's moist, ether-stained halls — He waits, hanging on the Tree, and sweats in you, as His gale fills your lungs and lips with an urge to art born of His unspoilt pulse. One can't leave Him, start to lay down a chart. Where two are, seek His inward earnest as food; carry the Other.

144. The Marble Body

Von Aschenbach sits, rigid, in a chair.
A bruised Apollo gazes at the sea,
then grants one final, glancing courtesy,
the blank eyes burning in his snaking hair.

And it is finished. Toppled in the sand,
he can no longer hear the greedy screams
of gulls in linen suits; miasmal dreams
engulf the empire of corrupted land.

The marble body cracks, as tendrils twine
across the deck and lick the mast like flames;
while senseless greenery dissolves all names
and sets him sail upon a sea-dark wine.

Young Dionysus shadows him through hell —
a polymorphous Proteus, whose fair
ringlets transform into the ruddy hair
of a ferryman who grunts: *I'll row you well.*

Ruddy ringlets, like flames, twine upon a toppled body—young Apollo. Then his marble courtesy cracks; miasmal wine dissolves him; the senseless hair, fair gazes, grunts in linen, engulf him, burning. While the sea (a ferryman of shadows), whose greedy tendrils lick at the rigid mast—hair snaking across the blank sail, glancing, in a row, through the dark suits of Proteus' deck—grants the polymorphous empire of dreams: land no longer, one sea, sets of eyes in the greenery. He sits, bruised, in the sand, and can hear the gulls. *All you well finished and corrupted names*! screams Von Aschenbach, *I'll transform into Dionysus, who is the final hell.*

145. Broken at the Feast

The wreck is anchored, honeycombed by worms.
It starts to rain: the cobbles opalesce;
the evening hitches up its rented dress;
gulls strut the crowded squares like football firms.

To drink another's vintage: sediment,
the lees of the Venetian underworld.
Unlike an argument this can't be willed;
receiving what you seemingly invent,

instead of proving you are rather proofed:
the milk of evening stirs the dormant yeast;
the loaves arise, are broken at the feast,
by fishermen and drunkards broken-toothed,

by this old woman, half her face a stain
as of spilled wine, who ravages the air,
raw as Galás reciting Baudelaire —
his miserere for the race of Cain.

Alas, you can't invent milk and honey. Dressed, combed by you, Cain airs the gull's strut. His fob tooth itches. The poor drink rain, fed the fig are a feast for worms. Arise, Woman, broken of old, receiving the crowded ravages of the underworld, who, rented by drunkards, stirs the lees of evening, its wreck anchored to the raw dormant *it*, yeast of the unlike. Another's sediment: face broken up by vintage argument, as *what* cobbles instead of loaves. The race half-starts, rather like this willed proving. We fisherman, in this naive net, as the spilled mere rises to stain squares at evening, reciting the blear adieu. Bely, *Thea* is near; Her seeming marsh atoll opalesces.

146. La Veneziana

...the dry, wrinkled fruit the gardener happened to find
remains the only riddle of this whole tale.
                                      —Nabokov

Moist oils catch Simpson's fluttering blue eye;
taut threads of canvas—like a racquet's strings—
suspend him, struck, between the world of things,
and *shuffling of unseen passersby.*

Reader, *respectful of another's grief,*
allow McGore to ply his instruments
in silence, solving to release the sense
of beeswax, myrtle, and quicksilver leaf.

The old procurer, wiping at his eyes—
the lynx fur slipping, and her glowing head—
congeals into the Keeper of the Lead.
The scent of lemon fades, the varnish dries.

Defenestrated: painter, lutenist
can only mock the garden where she steals,
the printed fruit the gardener conceals.
Smiling, the Bride adjusts her slipping mist.

The unseen oil Painter—instruments arc, wiping at the canvas of silence, to release the world, His blue Bride—conceals the glow in form's taut varnish. The mere procurer, of old steals Her sense. Moist mock-fruits catching her eye. Another, smiling, strings on the simp, slipping between mist. Gardens fade to only a scent, furl. Where the sad, fond lutenist plays, shuffling grief passes by on sad tender feet. His struck head slipping; gore congeals and dries. The Gardener printed the beeswax, suspends things like the fluttering leaf. She of quicksilver eyes leads the respectful reader in quest to Him; the just loving keeper of threads can allow of myrtle and lynx.

147. A Dangerous Encounter

On the small square, beside the jewellery box
of Santa Maria dei Miracoli,
tired of being lost intentionally,
you rifle through a store's discounted books

and, beneath Wimsatt's *Verbal Icon*, find
Jünger's *A Dangerous Encounter*.
Irene strays elsewhere. Is there cause to doubt her?
The thorns of yellow roses scratch the mind;

a single bruised bud peals its golden bell;
a perfume that should only skin adorn
diffuses like a portrait by Redon.
Outside: a body bleeding where it fell,

discreet retreats down gloomy corridors...
A fog-bound city is a chamber piece
for wind, stirred crowds, the whistles of police,
and screaming goddesses at hotel doors.

The dangerous city's intentionally stirred *jünger* wait. Crowds whistle at discounted goddesses. Outside the body — bound, bruised and bleeding elsewhere — discreet beneath golden skin, Irene finds a small store's single jewellery rifle, beside a bell, a box of yellow books. Tired police encounter screaming, down corridors of a lost hotel, where strays scratch doors. Thorns of doubts bud there, on verbal fog; a mist drones by *rami* loci. Roses adorn the wind for you Santa Maria. Her mind like perfume diffuses through the gloomy square chambers of being; the icon that fell pales, is only a portrait, a piece — it retreats to a cause; it should die.

148. The Same Motif

Dobrowsky judges that the expert thief
always employs the subtle force of thought,
and by his artist's signature is caught —
his oeuvre is haunted by the same motif.

Just so, in winter you may weave your nets
far from the bloody odour of the wharves,
the squares like palettes left by tired Fauves
beside unfinished paintings (delegates

in costume incarnate the perfect scheme
and gather, as anonymous as bees,
the dust of premature intimacies),
with tact ensuring that the crime scene seem

unchanged but for the facets you purloin,
to live a month like an aristocrat
hiding his cuffs, adjusting his cravat,
flipping an image like a tarnished coin.

The facets of His brow gather the sky. The just odour that scene left wavers like you, like thought hiding in a costume, an unfinished image haunted by an anonymous scheme. But His *is* is always incarnate as bloody intimacies, beside the thief moth, to purloin the tarnished — caught by force for a premature crime — from the subtle aristocrat in ashen-silk-cravat and cuffs, expert with winter palettes, the same tired motif that employs coin-flipping Fauves: ensuring dust may live. Far do His bees of seem-so, delegates of the unchanged, weave His signature, perfect the oeuvre. The Artist, adjusting nets, judges by tact — squares you and your paintings.

149. The Jumble Sale

As one come late, who finds the jumble sale—
which won't come round again for many weeks—
already stripped of labels and antiques
(a cheap Murano swan, a nightingale,

some athlete's memoirs...), I survey the pelf
others drag off across the treeless plain
towards the water nothing can contain,
having drunk which I contradict myself.

I had a plan, but now I'm not so sure.
The lottery is done, the lots are cast;
the masks are chosen, all except the last:
that of the person private and obscure.

There may be other, greater things to tell,
if we should pass, beneath Atropos' shears,
during the journey of a thousand years.
For now, just this: know I am doing well.

Beneath a thousand cheap labels and private masks, which are myself for sale, is just the greater person, stripped and obscure, I drag across plains of nothingless, towards a tree, the last one — the other's Other, already chosen to contain all things. If now a nightingale should tell of this journey, which having come to a pass, finds troops come that pare off ears, cast lots for antiques? Weeks half-drunk, doing the round again, athletes may mourn the late years. The memoirs of water contradict the plan we, who survey the many ajumble, can know. During the lottery, I swan but I'm not sure I am, except there be some I done well, won as the ashed Now.

150. His Other Body

Once having walked along the median street,
you have always already left your prints,
as if in concrete. While the little prince
who tries to tame you, skips on lighter feet.

Once having chosen from a thousand bars
this place to drink, you are already drunk.
Pandora cannot close her dusty trunk.
A *comet amongst calculated stars,*

one swerves aside, as if a teacher slipped
writing equations on a board with chalk;
passing the stations of a random walk,
he too must pass the jeering seconds, stripped

and scourged by restive subjects, not yet king
of all his realm; in mask and cloak conveyed,
the sunrise set to crown him still delayed,
his other body still awakening.

SANATORIUM:
1/3 ROSE STREET

1. A Mountain Cure

In Autumn you decided to forgo
Italian journeys for a mountain cure
among these ruins — city air, impure,
exchanging for the poverty aglow

in stoves where elders burn raw coal or waste,
and plumes are mingled with the fragrant mist
swaddling a stanza of the Akathist.
The priest, you find out, has exquisite taste:

in youth a poet, he admired the prose
of the strict Beckett, wrote on Leśmian, Klee.
But silence calls and we must give away
all that we have, and like the watchful crows

perch in the lavishly denuded boughs —
above a brittle trash of shields and crowns —
of trees that drag their worn, embroidered gowns
through smoke, renewing their schematic vows.

2. Abandoned Wards

The fridge is covered in magnetic words
when you arrive — or rather, I.
Disintegration plays on Spotify.
Shades shuffle, hoarsely, through abandoned wards.

Night spills crude oil into myriad drops.
Thus Darknes cleaved fast upon the backs
of Looking-Glasses, them illustrious makes.
The window, double-glazed, whose framing crops

the starless background — see your image sink
into the shallows of the other room...
built for consumptives... Countess von Colomb
persuaded Hermann Brehmer... leaking ink

upon your grazing fingertips that swirl the tain...
pages like ants raiding a plate of crumbs...
a kitchen lamp that ominously hums...
the freshness outside — darkness, stone and rain.

3. One More Round

A harsh light in the kitchen separates
the stacked and gleaming dishes from rest,
remaining to be washed. An endless test,
yet one more round of suds and greasy plates —

this moment smearing like a viscous sauce,
this poem smearing it across the page —
the mind of failure one acquires with age,
trapped in the outer suburbs of the Source:

wide streets, car dealership or chicken shop,
low chainlink fences, threadbare tennis courts,
a stoner boutique full of pipes and quartz,
the hell of memory. When will it stop?

Returning through the pines, the priest you met —
paint-stained and pushing, from the Orthodox
chapel, a barrow full of trash and rocks —
revealed your heart too dry, your eyes too wet.

4. The Perfect Work

Beside the reed-crowned pond, the autumn sun
is smoky weakness, swaddling pale yolk.
The present absence of the happy folk—
who fortunately linger at the dun

and rusting verge of vision—not by chance,
reflects gun-metal grey, the great machine.
Yet, on the fetid pond a stolen sheen
still bears the breath-prints of their breezy dance.

Here, shallows flow into exilic marsh,
or nile bend, where failed explorers gaze
upon the changeless ruin of their days.
The lead-lined sun is uniformly harsh

in its procession through the trees, incensed,
a waft of wrath, on which the light-boned birds
suspend their tintinnabulating words;
the perfect work is endlessly commenced.

5. A Festival of Failure

Loss, in the early dawn, crepuscular:
brown smoke unfolding from the chimneys stacks,
dark trees that bear upon their wind-lashed backs
a lead sky punctured by a pewter star.

Night, gnawing at its stitches, bares the wound
of the horizon, bloodily bedewed.
The image is, predictably, renewed.
A festival of failure, pines festooned

with rank effluvia of poverty
that haunt their evanescent ermine stoles.
Old men awaken, don their musty roles,
recalling childhood, rusting heraldry

they shuffled through to school. Their body shrinks,
exhaling perfume like a wilting spray;
skin turns to paper, as a cursive day
is written down in blood and other inks.

6. The Mushroom Pickers

The mushroom pickers, watchful as flâneurs,
discern between the toxic parasols
and the flamboyant; their attention crawls
among wet needles, over roots of firs,

as glossy as a beetle, then dissolves
in misty ambience. When evening falls
the forest echoes with the urgent calls
of clashing bucks. As lean as myth, the wolves,

pad silently, patrolling their terroir;
their silver nibs of fur in cursive write
on cool, blue airmail paper, to unite
the porous pack within a single spoor.

You tap the path ahead and fear to meet —
athwart the slick ascent — a form that could,
if threatened, drench with your astonished blood
the understorey green around your feet.

7. The Cinema

The smell of resin. Apodictic sun
briefly constructs a world — the potted plants
like paper cut-outs, while a young monk chants —
and then, by concrete clouds, it is undone.

Then secondary movers load antiques
(their off-white van is veiled in plastic tarps),
divans and footstools — while a poet larps
to be admitted to the wingéd cliques —

into the now abandoned cinema. The pose
assumed, a heavy curtain, may be drawn
aside to grant admittance to the dawn.
The cost of this remains translating prose.

The young Kieślowski rides a bicycle
across a postcard, framed and monochrome,
and keeps on riding infinitely home,
the reel unspooling, paradisical.

8. Hans Castorp

A middle-aged Hans Castorp, you retreat
where rusted pines and broken statuary
backdrop the shadows, in their finery,
who take the air on antiquated feet.

Half-hearted auditing of old debates,
and tepid glances into Kirghiz eyes...
Elsewhere, another hopeless conscript dies,
almost believing that he liberates.

Refugee children playing in the snow
or drawing hopscotch courts in coloured chalk...
Walking, you think of Alexander Blok:
Praying and weeping, though *wild winds would blow...*

the snows of winter... cover everything.
But snows of spring? Untimely nothingness,
like antidora for the priest to bless;
yet in this ermine, also, kneels the King.

9. Flakes of Skin

You walk along a virid colonnade,
beneath a trembling entablature;
the scales transform to powdered wings and stir,
receiving wafts of what the forest made

in some dark clearing — redolent of sap —
in which a beehive, called by semantron,
empties to gather meadow pollen. On
the rusting leaves each footstep leaves a trap.

The morning silence hears the young priest sing.
Beneath great folded wings, as green as grass
that never withers, burdened exiles pass
to sit beneath an icon, whispering.

The trembling of repentance. Flakes of skin
fall to the tiles — desiccated nouns.
Trees start to speak in leaves, wind stirs their crowns.
Yourself the sun now hammers golden thin.

10. Disfigured Statues

A spring day, thickly with a crayon daubed.
A tree, against which shadows fondly lean,
at noon, to shelter. Linger, in between.
Disfigured statues, in that absence robed,

await the ministrations of the moss
on mouldy pedestals; yet, grass surrounds
ruins and springs up from beneath all grounds—
always recovered from the snows of loss.

Remember? With a toothpick dipped in milk
you hid this once; now pages crease like skin.
The green has condescended to begin
within an amnion of bluest silk.

A lambent wind disturbs the pollen swarms,
and ruffles orders of imposing pines
so that they ring out, piercing, clear as tines.
Fragility is worshipped by the forms.

11. It Drifts Away

The mossy armchair rock and pine create
receives your drifting, in an idle wake,
beside the body of the forest lake —
it drifts away; you count the breaths and wait.

Nearby, a folly that neglect knocked up,
of stone; the flighty birds, atwitter, preen.
Naive sight paints a sentimental scene,
the clustered trees like brushes in a cup.

The onion dome shines, golden, in the pond —
where svelte ducks gather to accompany
the ritual procession: cloud and tree —
the day unfolding, tactful as a frond.

Outside another village bodies rot.
You read the Guardian. On the threshold black
sunflower seeds like teeth destroyed by lack.
Flags, scavenging, alight upon the spot.

12. Beyond All Storms

Asperged, the apples in a garden plot—
the village vacillates, becomings woods
here, at the edge, as moist, penumbral moods
beguile you, pausing by an empty lot—

inscribed by worms, hang clinging to the bowed
and mildew-powdered branches. Hard rain raps
against your beaded hood. Between the gaps,
a crystal discourse trickles; having flowed

beneath a guarded portal—flames of green
rippling on either side—it percolates
through mossy village huts, concrete estates,
as reminiscence tinctures the unseen

like blood in water, luring graceful forms
from crushing heights, and yet by modest bells
made meek. Each peal awakens broken shells,
as lightning shouts the peace beyond all storms.

Notes

Throughout the book, italics indicate quotations.

The opening epigraphs are from: Sergius Bulgakov, *The Bride of the Lamb*, trans. Boris Jakim (William B. Eerdmans, 2002); Régis Debray, *Against Venice*, trans. John Howe (Pushkin Press, 2013); an inscription on Jacopo de' Barbari's map, *View of Venice*.

The epigraphs to Part One are from: Sergius Bulgakov, *The Lamb of God*, trans. Boris Jakim (William B. Eerdmans, 2008); Plotinus, *Enneads IV*, trans. A.H. Armstrong (Harvard University Press, 1984); Owen Barfield, *Poetic Diction* (Wesleyan University Press, 1984).

In poem 3, "bound in no bouquet" is an allusion to Stéphane Mallarmé's "flower which is absent from all bouquets."

In poem 4, "almost Venetian" quotes the Wikipedia article on Ilya Repin's painting "Barge Haulers on the Volga."

In poem 6, "visionary dreariness" is from William Wordsworth, "The Prelude," XII, *Selected Poems* (Penguin, 1994)

In poem 11, "the end of the Chatterly ban" is from Philip Larkin, "Annus Mirabilis," *The Complete Poems* (Farrar, Straus & Giroux, 2012).

In poem 12, "delight in marble made to look like silk" is from John Ruskin, *The Stones of Venice* (De Capo Press, 2003).

In poem 18, "a folding picture post-card," is from Mary McCarthy, *The Stones of Florence and Venice Observed* (Penguin, 2006).

In poem 19, "annotated archipelago" is from Jennifer Scappettone, *Killing the Moonlight: Modernism in Venice* (Columbia University Press, 2014).

In poem 20, "Desires are already memories" is from Italo Calvino, *Invisible Cities*, trans. William Weaver (Harcourt Brace Jovanovic, 1978).

In poem 26, "your flesh is but the glass, which holds the dust," plays on a fragment from Joseph Brodsky, *Watermark: An Essay on Venice* (Penguin, 2013): "dust is the flesh of time."

In poem 28, "stands famished among all his pasts" is from Friedrich Nietzsche, *The Birth of Tragedy & The Genealogy of Morals*, trans.

Francis Golffing (Doubleday, 1956): "Man today, stripped of myth, stands famished among all his pasts and must dig frantically for roots, be it among the most remote antiquities."

In poem 32, "The war in Spain / brought us the charm of the Bolero," is from Kate Ferris, *Everyday Life in Fascist Venice* (Palgrave Macmillan, 2012).

In poem 39, "the old star-eaten blanket of the sky," is from T. E. Hulme, "The Embankment," *The Collected Writings of T. E. Hulme* (Clarendon Press, 1994).

In poem 50, "copy copies, all increase their kind" is from Yeats, "Supernatural Songs: II," *Collected Poems* (Vintage, 1992); "Motley cast down beside the marble stair" is from Francis Webb, "Middle Harbour," *Collected Poems* (UWA Publishing, 2011); "I think of cities: / Vicenza, Verona, Venice, clarities / enduring for a while beside some river," is from George Szirtes, "Venice," *Reel* (Bloodaxe, 2004).

The epigraphs to Part II are from: George Szirtes, "Venice"; Geoffrey Hill, "Al Tempo de' Tremuoti," *Broken Hierarchies: Poems 1952–2012* (Oxford University Press, 2013); R. S. Thomas, "Reflections."

Poem 71 contains quotes, some slightly altered, from the Venetian explorer Giovanni Miani, describing his expedition to find the source of the Nile.

The last quatrain of poem 73, is a very loose version of lines from Charles Baudelaire, "A Carcass."

In poem 92, "mask of state" is a quote, slightly altered, from one of Rilke's letters, in Birgit Haustedt, *Rilke's Venice,* trans. Stephen Brown (Haus Publishing, 2007): "A wonderful interpretation of the facade of the Doge's Palace occurred to me recently: it represents 'the mask of the state'... ".

In poem 97, "Your essence is in infinite regress" is from J. V. Cunningham, "The Phoenix," *The Collected Poems and Epigrams of J. V. Cunningham* (Swallow Press, 1971).

In poem 98, the fragments in italics are from Yeats, "Supernatural Songs, VIII."

The epigraphs to Part III are from: Tadeusz Różewicz, "Forms," *Selected Poems,* trans. Adam Czerniawski (Penguin, 19760; John Ashbery, *Self-Portrait in a Convex Mirror* (Penguin, 2009); Andrei Bely, "Symphony III - The Return," *The Symphonies,* trans. Jonathan Stone (Columbia University Press, 2021).

In poem 108, "where even the deceivers are deceived" is from Guy Debord, *Society of the Spectacle*, trans. Ken Knabb (Rebel Press, 1983): "The images detached from every aspect of life merge into a common stream in which the unity of that life can no longer be recovered. Fragmented views of reality regroup themselves into a new unity as a separate pseudoworld that can only be looked at. The specialization of images of the world evolves into a world of autonomized images where even the deceivers are deceived."

In poem 109, "undulating serpent," "wicket" and "peep show orifice" are from Henry James, *Italian Hours* (Penguin, 1995).

In poem 117, "a great star playing to an empty hall" is a play on a passage from Régis Debray, *Against Venice*: "But deprive Venice of its spectators, its extras, and it would decline and collapse in a week, its text dissolving, lost, haggard, like a great star forced to play nightly to an empty house."

In poem 124, "countries where it never rains" plays on a line from Jacques Brel's "Ne Me Quitte Pas."

Poem 131 draws on Sarra Copia Sulam, *Jewish Poet and Intellectual In Seventeenth Century Venice*, ed. and trans. Don Harrán (University of Chicago Press, 2009).

In poem 132, "a threshing floor behind it as it yields" is a play on a passage from Goethe, *Italian Journey*, trans. W. H. Auden (Penguin, 1992): "Now, at last, I have seen the sea with my own eyes and walked upon the beautiful threshing floor of the sand which it leaves behind it as it ebbs."

In poem 133, "When I read Goethe, I forget Bismarck" is quoted from Havelock Ellis, "Henry de Régnier," *North American Review*, vol. 201 (1915). The last quatrain is a play on lines from his poem "Water Feast."

In poem 135, I quote from Rilke's "Self Portrait."

In poem 137, "their purpose in the labyrinth of wind" is from Yeats, "Nineteen Hundred and Nineteen"; "Compounded of accidental phantasies" is from *The Collected Works of W. B. Yeats Vol. II: The Plays* (Simon & Schuster, 2010).

The epigraph to poem 141 is from Alessandro Marzo Magno, *Bound in Venice: The Serene Republic and the Dawn of the Book* (Europa, 2013).

In poem 145, "the lees of the Venetian underworld" is from Anthony Hecht, *The Venetian Vespers* (Atheneum, 1979).

In poem 146, all quotations are from Vladimir Nabokov, "La Veneziana," *Collected Stories* (Penguin, 2001).

In poem 150, "a comet amongst calculated stars," is from Sergius Bulgakov, *Philosophy of Economy*, trans. Catherine Evtuhov (Yale University Press, 2000).

In the final section, the quote in poem 2 is from Joseph Beaumont, "Psyche, Or Love's Mystery." The lines in poem 7 are from Alexander Blok, "98," *Poems of Sophia*, trans. Boris Jakim (Angelico Press, 2014).

Acknowledgements

Above all, I want to thank my dearest Kasia, and my family Maryla and Michael, for their love and support, during the writing of this book. Thanks also to Luke Fischer, for many years of true friendship and quickening conversation, and for his comments on the manuscript.

In addition, I'd like to thank those who've supported my poetry and have, in one way or another, contributed to this work: Chris Wallace-Crabbe, Stephen Edgar, Marco Fazzini, Robert Gray, Kevin Hart, Ellen Hinsey, John Milbank, Douglas Reid Skinner, Alex Skovron and George Szirtes. I am also indebted to David Bentley Hart, for his beautiful and illuminating books, and for agreeing to write the foreword to *Venetian Mirrors*. Finally, I want to honour the memory of Adam Zagajewski, whose poetry and generosity remain an inspiration to me.

While working on this book, I benefited greatly from time spent at the Château de Lavigny Writer's Residence, and at Hawthornden Castle. My thanks to everyone involved for the invaluable gift of time, unencumbered by the necessities of daily life.

Poems 25 and 52 were chosen, by Aidan Coleman, for publication in *Social Alternatives*, 41:4 (2022). The poems in the final section, "Sanatorium: 1/3 Rose Street," were shortlisted for the 2022 Newcastle Poetry Prize, and published in *The Anabranch: Newcastle Poetry Prize Anthology 2022*.

www.ingramcontent.com/pod-product-compliance
Lightning Source LLC
Chambersburg PA
CBHW031427160426
43195CB00010BB/646